Irene

Thank you for being in our life and for inspiring us to move to Nashville

Love
Sondra & Markus

Books By Sondra Ray

Birth and Relationships: How Your Birth Affects Your Relationships
Celebration of Breath
Drinking the Divine
Essays on Creating Sacred Relationships
Healing and Holiness
How to Be Chic, Fabulous and Live Forever
I Deserve Love
Ideal Birth
Inner Communion
Interludes with the Gods
Loving Relationships: The Secrets of a Great Relationship
Loving Relationships II
Pele's Wish: Secrets of the Hawaiian Masters and Eternal Life
Pure Joy
Rebirthing in the New Age
Rock Your World with the Divine Mother
The Loving Relationships Treasury
The Only Diet There Is

Sondra Ray and Markus Ray Online

LiberationBreathing.com publishes the most recent writings and creations by Sondra Ray and Markus Ray and serves as a community resource, providing information on seminars, trainings, private sessions, contacts, and practitioners available to you worldwide.

LIBERATION BREATHING

The Divine Mother's Gift

by

SONDRA RAY

with Markus Ray

Immortal Ray Productions

Nashville, TN

Copyright © 2014 by Sondra Ray and Markus Ray

All rights reserved. No portion of this book may be reproduced or utilized in any form or by any means, electronic or mechanical, including photocopying, recording, or by any information storage and retrieval system, without permission in writing from the publisher.

Immortal Ray Productions
3000 Vanderbilt Place #118
Nashville, TN 37212
www.ImmortalRay.com
ImmortalRayProductions@gmail.com

Liberation Breathing® is a U.S. registered trademark that is the intellectual property of Sondra Ray and Markus Ray. The name Liberation Breathing® may not be used in commerce, practice, or written material of any kind without the permission of the owners.

The contents of this book do not constitute medical advice. This book is intended as an informational guide. The practice and effectiveness of techniques and processes to achieve any desired results in the life of the student are the sole responsibility of the student. The remedies, approaches, and techniques described herein are meant to complement, and not be a substitute for, treatment and/or consultation with a qualified health care professional.

Editorial Supervision: Lia Schultz
Book Cover Design: Third Eye Studio – Heather LaCroix

Excerpt from "The Awakening of Universal Motherhood" reprinted with permission of Board of Amma.

Library of Congress Cataloging-in-Publication Data
Ray, Sondra

Liberation breathing: the divine mother's gift / Sondra Ray with Markus Ray
    p. cm.

ISBN: 978-0-9916277-0-7
1. Body, Mind & Spirit. 2. Self-Help: Affirmations. III. Family & Relationships.
I. Ray, Markus II. Title.

1st Edition, May 2014

ISBN: 978-0-9916277-0-7

Immortal Ray Productions

To you Divine Mother,

We bow before Your indescribable glory as the fount of all knowledge.
May everything we write be something beautiful for You.

Love,

Sondra Ray & Markus Ray

The great power that is Cosmic Maya, the Supreme Divine Energy,
the Mother Goddess embodies the totality of all there is to be known.
To worship the lotus feet of the Universal Goddess
gives human life its highest realization.

— Babaji

The air which we breathe is born of the breath of our Earthly Mother.
Man is the Son of the Earthly Mother,
and from Her did the Son of Man receive his whole body.
Your breath is Her breath.

— Jesus the Christ,
The Essene Gospel of Peace

Integrity

This book will introduce you to Liberation Breathing®, a powerful tool and practice for personal transformation. However, we stress the importance of practicing breathwork with a qualified practitioner. Reading this book by itself will not make you a Liberation Breathing® Practitioner or qualify you to be a Liberation Breathing® Instructor. For those new to the breathwork process, the first step is to begin 10 private sessions with a certified Liberation Breathing® Practitioner or a certified rebirther/breathworker. We recommend 10 sessions each with both genders of practitioners (a total of 20 sessions).

For those interested in receiving Liberation Breathing® sessions, go to the Liberation Breathing® website for more information on our certified practitioners. Before you begin your sessions with a breathwork practitioner it is appropriate to ask them about their background, training and qualifications for your own clarity and protection.

If you are already a rebirther/breathworker, reading this book does not qualify you to represent yourself as a Liberation Breathing® Practitioner, nor use the federally registered Liberation Breathing® name or logo in your practice. Nor are your authorized to teach to others this material without written permission from Liberation Breathing® and its owners. The name and the logo are the sole intellectual property of Sondra Ray & Markus Ray...and the Divine Mother. They reserve the rights to authorize their usage with those who have received the proper training and certification within their worldwide system of instruction. Rebirthers who wish to use Liberation Breathing® in their practice need additional training in matters of the Divine Mother.

Certified Liberation Breathing® Practitioners can be found on the Liberation Breathing® website: LiberationBreathing.com, as well as the criteria for becoming a certified Liberation Breathing® Practitioner. We welcome all inquiries at admin@liberationbreathing.com or from the "Contact Us" tab on the website.

To sponsor a Liberation Breathing® seminar or a Loving Relationships Training® in your area, go to "Contact Us" on the Liberation Breathing website and submit your request. The classes we offer around the world are listed under Events. You may also like to join our mailing list by submitting your name and email on the website. We look forward to your comments and inquiries.

Contents

Integrity ix
Acknowledgements xvi
Preface xvii
Introduction xix
O Mother of Fire xxi

Part 1: The Practice of Liberation Breathing

The Liberation in Breathing 1
The Evolution of Liberation Breathing 3
The Physical Dimension 4
The Mental Dimension 5
The Spiritual Dimension 6
Invoking the Divine in Liberation Breathing 7
Breathing with a Practitioner 8
The Breath Release 8
Stiffness, Tension, or Symptoms While Breathing 9
Superventilation Not Hyperventilation 10
Gentleness Leads to Pleasure 11
Wet Liberation Breathing 12
The Divine Mother's Gift 16
Receiving the Divine Mother's Instructions 17
The Divine Mother Names as a Meditative Practice 18
The 108 Names of the Divine Mother 18
Awakening the Divine Mother Energy 22
A Scientific Explanation by Eve Jones 23
Prana and Rejuvination—What the Mystics Say 25
Visual Recall—A Session in Pictures 27
Why Liberation Breathing Diverges from Other Practices 28
Liberation Breathing in a Group or Seminar 30

Part 2: The Experience of Liberation Breathing

Ricardo's First Liberation Breathing Experience 35
Markus and Madame Pele On the Big Island of Hawaii 40
Markus Chronicles A Liberation Breathing Intensive in Australia 41
An Obstetrician Discovers Birth-Day Consciousness.. 46

Part 3: Historical Landmarks of Liberation Breathing

My Path as a Healer 51
The Loving Relationships Training 52
Frederick LeBoyer: Birth Without Violence 53
LeBoyer and the Rebirthing Movement Influence Obstetricians 55
Meeting Babaji 57
Rebirthing and Waterbirth in Russia 60
Markus' Path to Liberation Breathing 61
How Liberation Breathing Evolved 65

Part 4: The Guiding Lights of Liberation Breathing

A Speech by Babaji 69
Babaji 70
The Mantra "Om Namah Shivay" 72
My Road To Babaji 73
The Divine Mother 76
Ammachi 78
The Words of Amma 81
Jesus and A Course in Miracles 83
Using A Course in Miracles 84
Overcoming Resistance to A Course in Miracles 88
Markus' Study of A Course in Miracles with Tara Singh 89
Morrnah Simeona: The Hawaiian Wisdom of Ho'oponopono 93
Ho'oponopono Experience in Hawaii 94

Part 5: Selecting or Becoming a Liberation Breathing Practitioner
- What Makes a Good Liberation Breathing Practitioner 99
- Training for the Liberation Breathing Practitioner 102
- A Checklist for Liberation Breathing Practitioners and Clients 103

Part 6: The Power of Processing Thoughts
- The Purity of Liberation Breathing 107
- Teachings on Purity from A Course in Miracles 107
- Affirmations 112
- Making Affirmations Work for You 112
- Self Esteem Affirmations 114
- Enlightenment through the Holy Spirit's Thought System 115
- Verbal Processing 117
- The Ultimate Truth Process for Self-Healing 119
- Louise Hay Explains The Mental Causes of Physical Illness 121
- Processing the Fear of Giving Up an Addiction 122
- Uncovering the Personal Lie 123
- Processing Heavy Emotions 129
- Anger and Its Consequences 130
- The Forgiveness Test 132
- A Tribute to Forgiveness—Markus' Birth Story 134

Part 7: Birth and Relationships
- The Biggies—Negative Consciousness Factors 137
- Relationship Patterns 138
- The Incest Pattern in Relationships 140
- The Birth Script in Relationships 142
- Conception Trauma and Affirmations 147
- Prenatal Trauma and Affirmations 149
- Infant Guilt and Affirmations 151
- Normal Birth 152

Unwanted, Unplanned, or Illegitimate Births 156
Wrong Sex at Birth 157
Previous Miscarriages, Abortions, or Fetal Death 160
Premature Birth 163
Caesarian Birth 166
Induced Birth 168
Breech Birth 171
Forceps Birth 173
Drugs at Birth 175
Conscious Conception and Ideal Birth 179
Conscious Pregnancy and Childbirth 181
Optimizing the Post-Natal Experience 184
Latest Ideas about Birth 186
The Divine Mother of Birth in Bali—Robin Lim 187
A Tribute to My Mother 188

Part 8: Ascension and Physical Immortality

The Unconscious Death Urge 193
An Outline of My Spiritual Healing Course 195
The Path of Ascension 200
Ascension and the Role of Liberation Breathing 202
Physical Immortality 203
Aliveness Affirmations 213
Babaji The Immortal Master 216
A Vow of Immortality 220
My Perspectives on Immortality 223
Dedication From Babaji's Cave 226
Ode #365: From the Tomb of Jesus to Babaji's Cave 231
Book List—Recommended Reading 233
About the Authors 241

Illustrations

Fig. 1. Divine Mother, Crestone, Colorado, Haidakhandi Universal Ashram i
Fig. 2. Hawaii's Kilauea Summit Caldera with View of Halema'uma'u Crater xxiii
Fig. 3. Liberation Breathing in Iceland's Blue Lagoon Thermal Waters 15
Fig. 4. Ricardo in the Ganges River during India Quest, Haidakhan 38
Fig. 5. Maria and Ricardo, India Quest, Haidakhan 39
Fig. 6. Babaji and Sondra Ray 59
Fig. 7. Babaji in Meditation 75
Fig. 8. The Divine Mother, Acrylic on Canvas by Markus Ray 79
Fig. 9. Christ by Heinrich Hoffman 87
Fig. 10. Tara Singh at Altar 91
Fig. 11. Morrnah Simeona 95
Fig. 12. Christ, Acrylic on Canvas by Markus Ray 111
Fig. 13. Sondra Ray at the Entrance of Babaji's Cave in Haidakhan, India 225
Fig. 14. Inside Babaji's Cave in Haidakhan 230
Fig. 15. Sondra Ray and Markus, Wedding Day in Haidakhan, April 4, 2009 232

Acknowledgements

We acknowledge the following Masters and Teachers who inspired us to write this book on breathwork and other important spiritual practices: Leonard Orr, the founder of Rebirthing; Sri Sri 1008 Babaji, our Master, the Maha Avatar of Haidakhan; Sri Muniraj, the "King of Silence"; Sri Shastriji, Babaji's High Priest; Sri Amritanandamayi, the Divine Mother in human form; Jesus the Christ, the Voice of *A Course in Miracles*; Dr. Helen Schucman, the scribe of *A Course in Miracles*; Tara Singh, Markus' teacher of *A Course in Miracles*; and Morrnah Simeona, Sondra's teacher of Hawaiian Ho'Oponopono. Through their guidance we have been blessed to live our lives in a sacred manner.

We give special thanks to Barbara Milbourn and Yvonne Perry for their invaluable editorial and technical help. We are most grateful for Lia Schultz for helping us bring this book and Immortal Ray Productions through the birthing process.

We give our heartfelt appreciation to all our organizers and Liberation Breathing® Practitioners around the world who help us in our global mission to spread these teachings and the good news of *Liberation Breathing: the Divine Mother's Gift*. We acknowledge all of the committed breathworkers around the world who have dedicated their lives to inspiring and healing themselves and others through the power of the breath.

Our photographer in London, Judy Totton, deserves accolades for all the portraits she has done for us in the past few years. She always makes herself available when we work in England, and always makes us look like our optimum selves. Thank You, Judy, for putting us in your lineup of "rock stars" whom you normally shoot.

Thanks for our website, LiberationBreathing.com, goes to Ned Horton, Ron Wagner, and the team of developers and representatives at Horton Group in Nashville.

Preface

Breath is Life. It seems obvious. Our breath is the most essential function of our life. But less obvious is that we use only a fraction of our breathing capacity. Therefore, let us consider that we are only a fraction alive.

Few have truly considered the relationship between healthy life and healthy breath. Sondra Ray has dedicated her life to this concept, and her new expression of this truth lies here in *Liberation Breathing: The Divine Mother's Gift*. Sondra Ray, with founder Leonard Orr, pioneered and helped to perfect a form of conscious, connected breathing called "rebirthing" in the 1970s. She has worked ceaselessly since then to spread the practice worldwide. Rebirthing saved people years of struggle by helping them discover and remove debilitating thoughts and memories that manifest as problems. It has led many to heal their lives through the power of their own breath. Through the breath people changed their lives by changing their minds. Through their breath they discovered a deeper inner peace, joy, and happiness.

It sounds too simple to say your breath can heal you; yet, it is simple, and that is exactly what it can do. Four decades later, Sondra Ray—one of the foremost experts on rebirthing as well as an international speaker and teacher on the subject of relationships—has been given a new expression of an inspirational healing process called Liberation Breathing®. This book is the flower of this new expression. It is for people who already have knowledge and experience of rebirthing, as well as for anyone who has never heard of using the breath for healing and inner self awareness.

Sondra Ray's passion for the breath as a healing tool and her devotion to the Divine Mother culminate in *Liberation Breathing: The Divine Mother's Gift*. It is destined to become the "bible" for her forty years of dedication to the breath as a means for transformation and healing, to relationships as a means for sacred living, and to spiritual Masters including Babaji, Jesus Christ, and the Divine Mother as our helpers for reaching realms of higher consciousness beyond our own thought processes or what we could achieve alone. You are invited into this world of the breath and its unlimited benefits. *Liberation Breathing* offers a new beginning to those who have never considered their breath as one of their most powerful healing assets. It offers further clarity to those who are familiar with the power of their breath to transform their lives.

As Sondra Ray's friend, creative director, co-author, personal poet, court painter, "ascension buddy," husband, and twin flame, I am happy to be part of this action. Liberation Breathing® is the ultimate cosmic bath. We breathe with you, our reader, in the possibilities of liberation in this lifetime, from all that prevents you from realizing perfect happiness and complete awareness of your true identity, and from death itself. It is our prayer that your own breath can take you to realms of inner peace you have naturally inherited, but until now have not known. It is our sincere invitation for you to know the liberation that your own breath provides, and to discover that *Liberation Breathing: The Divine Mother's Gift* can give you everything your true destiny promises.

—Markus Ray

Introduction

I went to the crater's edge on the Big Island of Hawaii today with my man to pray to Madame Pele like mad. I begged her to give me the beginning of this book. I had my offering in hand and was quite close to the edge when all of a sudden the land shook beneath my feet and there was an earthquake! We ran away from the edge immediately, and then Markus sat down and began to write Her a poem. It was appropriate she was speaking to us so loudly. After all, we had already decided to dedicate this book to the Divine Mother!

Nature can put you in an altered state. Poetry can put you in an altered state. People like altered states. *Isn't that why drinking, smoking, and drugs are so popular?* The Divine Mother's Liberation Breathing® puts you in an altered state without the risks and can, in fact, heal any harm done!

For those of you who are new to my books, I am glad to welcome you into this wonderful world of conscious, connected breathing, Babaji, and the Divine Mother. You probably have questions that this book can answer that relate to your own life, spiritual evolution, and self-identity. You might ask: *What is my divine purpose here?* and *What does my breath have to do with inner health and transformation?* Along the way you may also ask: *Who is Babaji? Who is the Divine Mother?* And, *What exactly is Liberation Breathing?* These are all the subjects of this book. I was absolutely guided to write it this way after visiting Madame Pele on the Big Island of Hawaii.

As I write this, I am sitting inside the screened porch of a house at the bottom of a lava flow. My words flow out in such a way that I cannot stop them and the land commands the new, the bold, and the latest. There is no other way here. On this island, new land is being formed as I speak. The volcanoes are actively belching steam and the cauldron is bubbling up. The land on the Big Island is so close to the Source. For that reason I have come here many times to get the first page of a book. I also check in with the kahunas (the Hawaiian spiritual masters) here, as I like to be aligned with them, especially when I am on the islands.

It was quite a while ago that the Divine Mother herself gave me the instruction to add certain components to this breathing process; and it has taken me some time to integrate exactly how to do that. Now it all makes perfect sense.

—Sondra Ray

O Mother of Fire

O Mother of Fire, Mother of Earth
Forming out of the Great Ocean,
To Thee I sing.

I place myself on the edge
Your Caldera—Kilauea—
The home of Your sleeping form,
Aroused and venting steam—
The belly of Your molten action.

You rumble under me—
A sign of Holy Nature.
I am grateful for so much power under me
So much mana
You infuse my body,
My soul,
The portion of Your crust I inhabit.
I am but a conglomerate of Your Holy dust
Liquefied and formed as human.
After all my uses complete,
Given back to You,
Transmuted as the ascended matter of immortality.

Holy Mother of Fire,
Light me
From the inside out.
Warm me with the molten being of Your Love;
Move as sacred substance inside the orb of my body;
Move Your Life Force within me, without me.

I ask Your direction.
I stand on the edge of Your earthen womb,
The Holy portal of Your potent presence.

Grip me,
Stun me into graceful submission.
Gladly I come running to Your Care,
Into the fires that
Burn my ego away.

Char my fears to nothingness,
Leaving only
Your fiery substance of courage
Flowing
Through my veins.

—Markus Ray

Part 1

The Practice of Liberation Breathing

The Liberation in Breathing

Why call this Liberation Breathing? The breath is the most essential aspect of our life. It has incredible healing properties. When used in such a way that it is conscious, deep, and connected, the benefits are not only more oxygen cleansing the cells of the body, but also greater energy of the life force—another name for the Divine Mother. Taking in greater life force cleanses the mind of its subconscious memories of hurt, anxiety, and conflict. By this method, you can be *liberated* from:

- pain
- negative thoughts
- tension or negative mental mass
- shallow breathing
- symptoms and disease
- fear
- anger
- guilt
- sadness
- the effects of traumatic incidents
- blocks to abundance
- addictions
- negative patterns in relationships
- birth trauma
- parental disapprovals
- unconscious death urges
- the past, including past lives
- false religious theology and dogma
- depression
- the ego

You can even be liberated from death! In her book *The Path of Empowerment* Barbara Marciniak explains that "awareness and control of the breath are the essential keys for understanding and developing the higher mind because they form a very powerful and natural way to connect with both inner and outer sources of vital life force energy." Marciniak notes that you can use your breath to:

- stabilize yourself
- have more energy
- enhance your immune system
- create beneficial brainwave patterns
- travel into the interior of your being
- acquire transcendent knowledge and information
- seek higher consciousness

Through our facilitation of thousands of sessions around the world, we regularly observe that Liberation Breathing® results in:

- more bliss in daily life
- more pleasure in your physical body
- increased physical energy
- life becoming more effortless and fun
- the ability to breathe freely and naturally
- work becoming more like play
- a dimension of spiritual energy which you may not have experienced
- the ability to receive love and have the direct experience of letting it in
- increased psychic awareness
- more experiences of telepathy and intuitive knowledge
- transformations in physical appearance and beauty
- a propensity for youthfulness and a desire for longevity
- improved prosperity (letting go of the "there is not enough" mentality)
- enhanced creative ability
- greater personal connection to infinite intelligence
- seeing the truth of your hang ups and ways to clear them
- rising self esteem

Clients tell us all the time about miraculous transformations. We believe the benefits of Liberation Breathing® are endless. *Accelerate your growth! Try it!* It is a very effective process to solve problems, free yourself from the past, and get in touch with yourself in a very deep way. It also gets you directly in touch with your *inner guidance*, or *higher self*, which may have been dormant. In short, Liberation Breathing® wakes you up. Krishna said, "Words cannot describe the joy of the soul whose impurities are cleansed. Only those who feel this joy know it!" Liberation Breathing® gets you in touch with that joy!

The Evolution of Liberation Breathing

We hope we have whetted your appetite and aroused your curiosity. You must be wondering what Liberation Breathing® really is and how it evolved. Liberation Breathing® was born out of the very gentle and compassionate process called rebirthing. It is conscious, connected breathing—a physical, mental, and spiritual experience all in one. It uses all of the knowledge and research of rebirthing from the past 40 years while deepening the spiritual elements of the practice.

This conscious, connected breathing method was originally called rebirthing because any conscious breathing can stimulate birth memories—the moment of the first breath. When some hear the word "rebirthing" they begin to release fears from birth that remain suppressed in the body. It is such a *relief*! We hope to enlighten you and dispel myths and misinformation once and for all. There is nothing to fear. Rebirthers all over the world have helped thousands of people clear up their lives by the use of simple means: facilitating an hour of deep, connected breathing in the upper chest; changing negative patterns of thinking; breathing out stuck energies in the body; and breathing in greater amounts of life force.

Liberation Breathing® is our new expression of conscious, connected breathing that invokes the Divine Mother energy into each session. The spiritual elements of Liberation Breathing® bring an awareness to both the breather and the practitioner of the *life force* at work that transcend the conscious effort to change one's life and mind. This new enhancement is a tremendous gift and we are happy to be the ones given this responsibility. What a privilege! We were entrusted with this process, instructed to register the name, and oversee the quality of all Liberation Breathing® practitioners.

The Physical Dimension

In Liberation Breathing® the inhale and exhale are connected in a relaxed rhythm, pulling the inhale up into the upper chest—into the heart center or sternum area—and relaxing totally on the exhale. The inhale and exhale merge so that breathing feels and sounds like an unbroken circle. The inhale and exhale are relaxed and full, not forced. The breathing is not too fast or too slow. The most important aspect is the rhythm. One can breathe in and out through the mouth or in and out through the nose. We prefer that people start breathing through the mouth so we can hear the breath well, and so clients get a full-on experience. Breathing through the mouth also allows a larger intake of air and energy. This kind of breathing is done mostly in the chest, with emphasis on breathing with the lungs instead of the diaphragm or belly, which has a different purpose.

The rhythmical, circular breathing, done by pulling on the inhalation and relaxing on the exhalation in a continuous, connected stream, empties the negative mental mass from the body and enables you to incorporate life energy into your body. At some point, there is a reconnection to Divine energy, and, as a result, you may experience tingling and vibration in your body. This is good! It means old darkness is going out and new energy is moving in! This new, universal energy vibrates out tension and pain, which is the manifestation of negative mental mass.

This breath cycle into the upper chest can break you out of unconscious holding patterns in regard to breathing and living. It is like a baptism of the Holy Spirit with power. The breath, together with raising the quality of your thoughts, can heal almost anything.

The Mental Dimension

Liberation Breathing® is not only deep, consciously connected breathing in the upper chest, it is an introspective observation of our thoughts. It is a practice of constantly looking at the content of our own mind in order to empty out the negative thought forms that are ultimately causing us distress in life. It is a means of taking 100 percent responsibility for all experiences that show up in our life now, and have ever shown up in our past life, or will show up in our future life yet to be. It is the beginning of a state of mind that aspires to be free of all conflict and judgment. Liberation Breathing® has the potential to liberate us from the consequences of thought itself, and place us back in the Mind of God from which we came.

The Liberation Breathing® process helps us look at our thoughts and memories and uncover the causative mental factors that produce our life's results. Millions of bits of data are producing effects each second in our minds. Yet, we are aware of so few of them. *How do we cleanse ourselves of the negative and destructive bits?* At some point we become aware of the subconscious mind activating experiences, and the need for the help of the Divine to clear these unconscious factors. Without the help of a forgiving Divine Intelligence, this clearing would be next to impossible. Therefore, we have taken the step to "hand over" the process to the Divine Mother—to a super consciousness factor.

Breathing in this productive way is a potential you have always had. However, most people sub-ventilate, perhaps due to unconscious fears of stimulating early memories as far back as birth. Liberation Breathing® makes it safe for these memories to come up, if they do. The LB® practitioner will help you release them from your body and help you change any negative thoughts associated with these memories. In my experience, it always feels better to release these memories than to keep them suppressed. Suppressing them gives them more energy and causes pain, negative symptoms, and disease. Releasing them brings health.

The Spiritual Dimension

The spiritual dimension of Liberation Breathing® is the heart of the matter. Connecting the inhale to the exhale merges spirit with air. It merges the Divine energy with the physical body in a way that nourishes the nervous system; it cleans the blood and relaxes the organs as well as the mind. This spiritual breathing is like a biological experience of God. The yogis of ancient times referred to this energy as prana. It is more than just air intake; it is a "spiritualized" breath that is the source of life itself. It is the very energy of existence—the Divine Mother's most essential blessing. It makes life in a body possible.

The purpose of Liberation Breathing® is not just the movement of air, but also the movement of energy. Maintaining a relaxed, connected breathing cycle for a few minutes will begin to produce dynamic energy flows in your body. These energy flows are the merging of spirit and matter. The level of your own spiritual enlightenment and the intuitive guidance of your LB® practitioner is the biggest factor in determining the power of your energy flows. Breathers often experience energy flows as tingling or vibrating sensations in the body. When these energy flows happen, your body is filling with pure life energy and light; your mind and body are being cleansed of tension and impurities.

Working with conscious affirmations to change one's negative thoughts are essential to the Liberation Breathing® process. *But what liberates us from the vast reservoir of negative thoughts held in the subconscious mind?* It takes something far beyond conscious thought and breath alone. The Divine Mother energy, the pure *shakti power* of the Holy Spirit, is needed to make a radical change. It is Divine intervention for counteracting entrenched tendency. What the conscious mind does not "catch" as the culprits of negative experiences, the Divine Mother of the Holy Spirit roots out and neutralizes in Her active compassion. This is why the Divine Mother has instructed a "calling in" through prayers and mantras of a *Life* force, making the session nine times more powerful (according to our clairvoyants) for handling the vast subconscious factors of our self-sabotaging thoughts and memories, accumulated over life times. As practitioners, we have witnessed the incredible, often miraculous results of this added invocation.

Spiritual purifications techniques such as honoring the five elements of fire, air, water, earth and space are used by many rebirthers. These techniques are helpful to the mental and physical cleansing. By adding the dimension of prayers and mantras from the Divine Mother, people feel safer and go deeper while receiving all the support of the Mother.

Invoking the Divine in Liberation Breathing

Today, we are continuously improving Liberation Breathing®. It is a very pure and powerful process of spiritual transformation that can totally change a person's life—even their destiny. We are clear that the *power* of one's own breath can do this, being the catalyst for true inner change. Miracles in one's life can and do happen, through the insights gained in breathing in this circular, connected way.

Liberation Breathing® works on its own, therefore we do not mix other modalities in with it. People get in touch with the *power* of their own breath—one of their greatest healing assets. Yet, we find that people need help to overcome addiction to negative thoughts and conditioning. To clear and cleanse thought itself, we seek help outside the system. This is why we invoke the Divine Mother and the Divine Father energies as an essential part of each session—to help us let go. Liberation Breathing® takes a person beyond thought itself, into the realm of Holy thoughts or miracles.

In India they say the original spark of creation is a feminine aspect. The Divine Mother is the Primordial Power, the Creative Energy. But in order for anything to actively come into manifestation we also need the Divine Father energy. One could say the Divine Mother is the *in breath of God* and the Divine Father is the *outbreath of God*. They are two sides of a coin. We invoke the Divine Father by working with our Master Babaji's energy in each session. He is also in constant communion with Christ. Since we always incorporate *A Course In Miracles* into the work, we have the Christ energy as well.

Toward the end of the private Liberation Breathing® sessions, we read "The 108 Names of the Divine Mother" to bring in the purity and help of the Divine Mother while the person is still breathing. Then we have the client turn on his or her side for the closing, and we recite a special mantra in Sanskrit to the Divine Mother to further invoke Her healing powers. The client does gentle nasal breathing during this part (whereas the rest of the session is open-mouth breathing). The client breathes in a special rhythm, synchronized with the reciting of the 108 mantras of the Divine Mother. This, our latest guidance, sets in place the high intentions of the session, and invokes a spiritual energy that aids the breather to let go of the past. After reading the names and reciting the mantra, we experience a strong presence of stillness and silence that is profound for us and the client as well. This adds to the purity of the Liberation Breathing® session.

Breathing with a Practitioner

Breathing in the presence of a LB® practitioner gives you tremendous self-healing power. And, when your LB® practitioner knows you are ready, you can learn to do a full cycle solely by yourself. We do not recommend trying this breathing process alone in the beginning. It is possible to experience tenseness in the hands and get stuck without help. It is possible to go into an infancy memory pattern and not know how to get yourself out. These conditions are easily overcome with a practitioner, and understood to be just passing phases of the breathing process. Taking in a tremendously increased level of oxygen and energy—but not burning it up with exercise, such as jogging—is very cleansing and activating to the system. It infuses the body with a power we are not used to; therefore, it is wise to experience it in the presence of a trained practitioner. If you want to have a little taste of the benefits on your own, begin by doing ten connected breaths as described above.

The Breath Release

If you stick with Liberation Breathing®, eventually, you will remember your first breath. It is important to continue your breathing practice until this happens. The moment when it occurs is called a *breath release*. It will happen only when you feel safe enough to remember and re-experience your first breath. The breath release is the turning point, because in that moment, the breath mechanism is healed of the damage done to it at birth.

Prior to a breath release, people usually breathe by taking in very little air on their inhale and forcing the exhale. This does not promote longevity! The cells crave oxygen, while exhaustion and old age set in from forcing the exhale.

After a complete breath release, a person breathes differently. There is a natural pulling in on the inhale and a relaxing on the exhale. During a breath release it actually feels like someone else is breathing you. God is taking over and it is exhilarating. People often have mystical experiences during this release. The only thing to do at that moment is to surrender and thank God you are being healed.

Stiffness, Tension, or Symptoms While Breathing

Sometimes during breathing sessions one may experience symptoms like stiffness of the hands. This is due to releasing suppressed tensions accumulated and stored in the brain during infancy; and, mostly, it is due to resisting the life force entering the body. It is also caused by forcing, or blowing, on the exhale. As LB® practitioners, we never worry about this as it is absolutely temporary resistance, and when one keeps on breathing, the breath will take out the resistance. People who have the ability to let go quickly do not usually experience this. Those that let go, find it amazing that they can change their bodies and get themselves out of resistance. We discover the negative thoughts they are hanging on to; and when they let go of that, the hands let go.

A symptom is a manifestation of an old negative thought or memory and can be released through the breath. Symptoms take varied forms, including:
- pressure on the body parts as one remembers coming down the birth canal
- remembrance of the "unlimited sadness of the human condition" that infants sometimes experience (due to mishandling or birth-related trauma)
- the smell of anesthesia as it comes out of the cells

Symptoms appear and disappear in a matter of minutes. *All symptoms are actually the cure in process.* All one has to do is maintain connected breathing and follow the guidance of the practitioner who has already been through these experiences and has certainty that they are temporary. Your body is trying to spit out an old thought. It is better to go through a few minutes of symptoms in a session and breathe them out than it is to suppress negative thoughts which can result in negative mental mass, tension, and disease.

Symptoms are rarely painful unless you make them real and fight them. They are thoughts that *you* can change. Most people, in fact, think of these dramatic psycho-physical memory phenomena as interesting and even fun. Your breath and spirit gently release the symptom from your mind and body and you feel free and clear.

Superventilation Not Hyperventilation

In the following paragraphs, drawn from *An Introduction to Rebirthing for Health Professionals,* Dr. Eve Jones explains the differences between the rebirthing or Liberation Breathing® breath and the occurrence of hyperventilation:

"Such a pattern of breathing is *not* hyperventilation. It is simply a pattern that allows the individual to breathe all the time, not just for part of the time. It opens up previously unused lung space, so it can be called *superventilation*. Because the exhale is not forced or prolonged, there is none of the excessive blowing off of CO_2 that is the cause of Hyperventilation Syndrome.

"Hyperventilation occurs when the partial pressure of CO_2 in the blood circulating to the brain stem is so low that it is below the threshold for stimulation of the inspiration center located in the brain stem. The center thus doesn't trigger off another inspiration until the partial pressure of CO_2 accumulates and passes the threshold value. As the person who has been blowing out forcibly feels breathless during the long pause before the CO_2 builds up, he experiences a psychological state we call panic. And in his panic, he pushes himself to take another breath and then pushes even more on the next exhale, thus compounding the problem. The acid/base balance in the blood stream adjusts to the lowering of the CO2 and a condition known as alkalosis develops, characterized by tetany and muscular spasm, often to the point of producing intense pain in the strained muscles and joints.

"Tens of thousands of perfect breathing sessions have been conducted without the client getting involved in hyperventilation. But, it is true that people who are afraid of the feelings and thoughts within them start to push on the exhale, as if they were ridding a body of something bad. The less relaxed a client is about the entire process, the more likely he is to suffer the inconveniences of hyperventilation. As the client moves through the spastic phase, he learns that he can let go, and he stops hyperventilating in the face of stress.

"In short, the *superventilation* of the breathing process appears to cure the hyperventilation attack and makes it no longer necessary for the person to create it again. Any apprehension you may have had because of confusing the breathing process with hyperventilation can be discarded."

—Dr. Eve Jones

Gentleness Leads to Pleasure

The key to success in conscious breathing is softness and gentleness. Liberation Breathing® is 99 percent pleasurable. The one percent of Liberation Breathing® that is not enjoyable is an unwillingness to give up misery. Really! All discomfort in conjunction with Liberation Breathing® comes from holding on to negativity, misery, or pain.

People usually tell us, "It is far more wonderful than anything you said." God's energy can heal all human problems. Your breath is your direct link to this energy. Liberation Breathing® is the science of letting in God's energy, wisdom, and love. It is a real spiritual gift. It is possible to be filled with serenity, joy, health, and spiritual wisdom. Liberation Breathing® actually delivers more of these things than we can promise.

The Liberation Breathing® experience varies from person to person and from session to session. For all of you who have ever dreamed of being reborn and starting life all over again, you can now make that possible! *Wouldn't you like to free yourself from tension and stress? Wouldn't you like to overcome long-standing symptoms and old memories of trauma? Wouldn't you like an effective way to release pain and disease, even letting go of your family conditioning around death?* For one who has gone through the process, experiences of huge shifts usually happen:

> Dear Sondra and Markus,
>
> Thank you for the Liberation Breathing weekend in Houston about six weeks ago. Something changed inside of me that weekend. My life has become much happier. I just want you to know how thankful I am for the work that you do. I had been trying to make this change for some time. It was a gift for me to participate in the Loving Relationships Training and experience the power of my own breath.
>
> —Love, Nancy A. Houston, TX

Wet Liberation Breathing

The benefits of wet Liberation Breathing® are beyond the beyond, for a number of reasons. Wet breathing puts you back in the womb! While in the liquid environment of the womb, you were totally in a *world of your own*, protected from the outside, absorbed by your mother, and alone with your thoughts. You can experience the bliss, as well as the fears, of your earliest life in this incarnation. It is truly remarkable as a catalyst for bringing to the surface thoughts and memories that have been suppressed since your actual womb time.

Many people re-experience the relationship they had with their mother in the womb, and get even clearer on the decisions they made, the "core beliefs" they formed, and the "personal lie" they acquired during their whole conception-prenatal-birth-postpartum period of life, also known as the "birth script." Wet Liberation Breathing® is the fastest way for a person to clear the birth script formed in early life and carried around since the moment of conception.

For some there is fear involved with wet Liberation Breathing®. I assure you, having been a Registered Nurse for 14 years, I would never dedicate my life to anything that is not life enhancing and free of any danger. But even so, people may still have some fear. Snorkel breathing *under water* for an extended period of time may be confronting, especially in a tub, where the body is confined. This can bring up claustrophobia in some.

A good practitioner can assist you in quickly moving through these fears, and the benefits will be astounding. You will clear these toxic memories from your birth script very quickly. In fact, some of these suppressed fears, already in your subconscious, will be *permanently* released after one session of wet Liberation Breathing®. That is the whole purpose of Liberation Breathing®—to liberate your mind from fear resulting from memories held from your past.

Once you are in the water, have adjusted to the snorkel, and have gone through a couple rounds of letting go your most fundamental fears, you will find the "bliss factor" from wet Liberation Breathing®. Especially in thermal waters, there is an expansiveness of the soul that people experience from totally letting go and trusting that *Life* is on their side, and anything is possible. Liberation Breathing® helps a person really get that *Life* is an opportunity of endless possibilities, benevolence, and love.

When a person joins their will with the Universal Will of Creation, this combination is unleashed as a power of *Love* that is unstoppable and can create anything. A person who experiences this in a wet Liberation Breathing® session, if only for five seconds, will never be the same again. The inner transformation is remarkable. I have seen it. People walk away as *a new person*, freed from the debilitating memories of the past that were "lodged" in the subconscious, unexamined and unreleased.

The *grace* of wet Liberation Breathing® is a mystery, yet a demonstrable result I have witnessed over and over again in my 40 years of practice as a breathworker. People definitely are *reborn* into a new life on the cellular level, as the process of breathwork clears the cells of the memories of toxic thoughts that are held there. Memory, thought, and experience all form a "physical thing" held in the cells themselves. Until they are cleansed through some sort of spiritual purification technique like Liberation Breathing® or a radical forgiveness process, the cells cling to these negative memories, or "charges," affecting the actual physical evolution of the organism. Negative memories contribute to actual physical symptoms and disease. Wet Liberation Breathing® is the most effective process of spiritual purification and the fastest I know of to clear away the negative "valence" of the cells carried over from the trauma of the birth script. With the new possibility of neutralizing the toxic memories of the cells and releasing negative thoughts, a person has the opportunity to live and rejuvenate the body to perfect health and longevity through Liberation Breathing®.

Breathing consciously, as we do in this process, is more important to sustaining life than consuming food. What the ancient yogis call *prana*—a combination of atmosphere, light, and life force—is the most essential element to the sustenance of *you* in this physical universe. Next essential is water. Water is the "nectar of Life." Combined with the air element in wet Liberation Breathing®, you can literally rejuvenate your system into a dynamo of Divine Will. *What could be better?* Just you and the Divine Mother energy of light, air, and water is all you need…coupled with the spiritual practice of wet Liberation Breathing®. Then, *boom*, an unstoppable version of *you* climbs out of the waters into a new immortal life! This is the ultimate of spiritual purifications—a love bath of the Holy Spirit.

Each year we offer wet Liberation Breathing® Intensives in the thermal waters of Iceland's Blue Lagoon and at sites around the world such as the thermal baths of Caldes de Montbui, Spain and Budapest, Hungary—the thermal spa "capital" of Eastern Europe. The full experience of wet Liberation Breathing® involves breathing underwater with a series of personalized prayers. I cannot imagine anything more wonderful, as it comes from The Divine Mother Herself. People have many miracles. You can experience wet Liberation Breathing® for yourself with a certified practitioner in a hot tub, bathtub, warm pool, or thermal spring.

The Divine Mother's Gift

Liberation Breathing® is very, very sacred. When I started rebirthing in 1974, I did not fully understand it. I thought it was some kind of scientific process. I thought it was a treatment to heal my birth trauma. Now with the evolution of the entire process, I have been instructed to call it "The Divine Mother's Liberation Breathing®" because it is like a sacrament. You partake of the Holy Spirit. It is the mind of the Divine Mother, Babaji, and Jesus—the dream team!

It is really like making love to God. It is also God making love to you. It is all about *life*. It is *life giving*. It brings *youthing*. It brings healing. It brings joy. It has brought me everything I wanted. To me it is the ultimate gift from God. It is *drinking the Divine*. It is the everlasting nectar of immortality. It is discovering the fountain of youth. It is the gentle breath of bliss and the power of vitality charging the body. It is the thrill of thrills and the serenity of peace at the same time. It is the ultimate cosmic bath.

Liberation Breathing® is literally for everyone. No matter who you are or where you are on the path, it will take you higher than you ever thought you could go. You will eventually enter the banquet hall of eternity. You will wonder how you ever lived without it. Your heart will awaken with eternal passion. We personally think it is something you will want to do for life.

Liberation Breathing® merges the inner and outer breath, creating a bridge between the physical and spiritual dimensions. This connection unites the human body to the prenatal life energy that built it originally, and thereby rejuvenates the body and frees the individual consciousness from any kind of trauma, including birth trauma. It is an experience of opening your breath so that a special flow of spiritual energy washes the mind and body with a divine bath. It is the science of letting in the Divine Mother's energy, wisdom, and love to better experience the fullness of Divine energy in the physical body.

Receiving the Divine Mother's Instructions

A decade ago, as I was leaving Babaji's ashram in India, his High Priest Shastriji handed me a sheet of paper. At the top was a title: "The 108 Names of the Divine Mother." I had no idea why he gave it to me, or what to do with it. I landed in Stockholm, arrived at my hotel room, and set up my altar for my usual spiritual practice. I decided to read the "108 Names" from the paper out loud in front of my pictures of Babaji and the Divine Mother. Afterward I remained still and meditated. Suddenly, I received the most incredible knowledge! I was instructed to do an advanced wet breathing technique under water. I grabbed my snorkel and nose plug, jumped in my hotel bathtub, and tried the technique underwater. But, I found it to be very, very challenging. I spent five days mastering the technique. Then, I received the message that *The Liberation Training* for this wet breathing technique should be done in thermal mineral springs, as *that* was the real Divine Mother!

Soon after, I decided to try the technique out on another great healer, Don McFarland, founder of Body Harmony. He came flying out of the water shouting: "*This* is a stroke of *genius*!" I replied, "It is not from me. It is *direct* from the Divine Mother." I knew it was a miracle—the Divine Mother's gift.

Don and I spoke about how we could try the technique in thermal waters. I told him about the healing properties of the Blue Lagoon in Iceland. I had read about a movie director with psoriasis who had tried everything to heal yet nothing worked. Eventually, he travelled to the Blue Lagoon in Iceland, immersed himself in the thermal waters, and healed entirely. Don and I decided to take a group to Iceland to try the technique. I am grateful that he helped me organize the first trip as it was all new to me, and I needed support. The group was blown away—both by the technique and by Iceland. It was so powerful that it took me quite some time to integrate the whole experience.

The Divine Mother Names as a Meditative Practice

You are invited to incorporate the Divine Mother Names into your daily prayer and meditation practice. Before reciting, prepare an offering of fresh or silk flower petals. Sit in the lotus position in front of your altar with an image of the Divine Mother (Mother Mary, Amma, Quan Yin, Lakshmi, or to whomever you most relate). Light a candle and a favorite scent in offering to the Divine Mother.

Begin the ceremony by speaking out loud: "Om, I bow to her, the mother of the universe." Before each line, repeat, "Om, I bow to her…" If you join with others in a group, speak each line in unison and provide a copy of the names to each participant. The word *Swaha* means "I offer myself." When you say "Swaha," toss a petal onto the altar in front of the Mother's picture.

Shastriji said, "Embody these qualities of the Mother in yourself." As you recite, take the actual sound vibration and the meaning of the words into your heart.

The 108 Names of the Divine Mother

Om, I bow to Her,

1. The Mother of the universe…Swaha
2. Who resides in the heart of the Master…Swaha
3. Who gives birth to the worlds…Swaha
4. Who is full of boundless mercy …Swaha
5. Whose form is blissful…Swaha
6. Who is worshipped by the worlds…Swaha
7. Who is the supreme Goddess…Swaha
8. Who is the Mother as a warrioress…Swaha
9. Who bestows good fortune…Swaha
10. Who is divinely beautiful…Swaha
11. Who is the embodiment of knowledge…Swaha
12. Who is prosperity…Swaha
13. Who sustains all the world…Swaha

14. Who is the Goddess of heaven...Swaha
15. Who reads all minds...Swaha
16. Who gives victory to her devotees...Swaha
17. Who is divine energy...Swaha
18. Who is worshipped by divinities...Swaha
19. Who looks after the universe...Swaha
20. Who removes all fear...Swaha
21. Who gives divine protection...Swaha
22. Who is the Goddess of the waters...Swaha
23. Who fulfills all desires...Swaha
24. Who is the Mother of the three worlds...Swaha
25. Who gives liberation...Swaha
26. Who is the Goddess of fortunes...Swaha
27. Who resides in the lotus...Swaha
28. Who is worshipped by God...Swaha
29. Who is full of Power...Swaha
30. Who removes the troubles of the universe...Swaha
31. Who gives birth to all...Swaha
32. Who is the consort of victory...Swaha
33. Who is of royal majesty...Swaha
34. Who is the Goddess of Gods...Swaha
35. Who resides in the heart of the king of sages...Swaha
36. Who showers the nectar of grace...Swaha
37. Who is the power of consciousness...Swaha
38. Who is the maker of destiny...Swaha
39. Who is beyond all things...Swaha
40. Who is full of mercy...Swaha
41. Who is the Goddess of the planet...Swaha
42. Who is the Goddess of perfection...Swaha
43. Who is the power of the beginning...Swaha
44. Who resides in Jerusalem...Swaha
45. Who is inaudible sound...Swaha

46. Who is supreme might…Swaha
47. Who is energy everlasting…Swaha
48. Who is knowledge of the beyond…Swaha
49. Who is glorified by the scriptures…Swaha
50. Who is indestructible…Swaha
51. Who is the great fighter…Swaha
52. Who is transparent like a crystal…Swaha
53. Who breathes as the children…Swaha
54. Who breathes as the children…Swaha
55. Who breathes as the children…Swaha
56. Who showers the nectar of love…Swaha
57. Whose every organ is the source of light…Swaha
58. Whose nature is joyful…Swaha
59. Whose voice is most sweet…Swaha
60. Who is praised by perfected souls…Swaha
61. Who is the power of the origin…Swaha
62. Who removes all pain…Swaha
63. Who crushes pride as the enemy…Swaha
64. Who heals all wounds…Swaha
65. Whose light shines as the full moon…Swaha
66. Who accepts all surrender…Swaha
67. Who is sacrifice…Swaha
68. Who is the principle power…Swaha
69. Who is the power of Om…Swaha
70. Who is divine sound and light…Swaha
71. Whose body is the universe…Swaha
72. Who resides in the heart of Hairakhandi Shiva…Swaha
73. Who is Tara, destroyer of the dark force…Swaha
74. Who is the Goddess of the Goddesses…Swaha
75. Who gave birth to the Savior…Swaha
76. Who is the embodiment of mercy…Swaha
77. Who is without blemish…Swaha

78. Who protects the three worlds…Swaha
79. Who gives shelter to all…Swaha
80. Who is the embodiment of divinity…Swaha
81. Who is the enchantress of all…Swaha
82. Who is the Mother of fire…Swaha
83. Who removes poverty and misery…Swaha
84. Who gives nutriment and plenty…Swaha
85. Who is the breath of the wind…Swaha
86. Who is the object of meditation…Swaha
87. Who annihilates all fear…Swaha
88. Who is praised by both Gods and demons…Swaha
89. Who is the queen of the battlefield…Swaha
90. Who holds the rosary, conch, and flower…Swaha
91. Who shines like the stars…Swaha
92. Whose glory is sung by Brahma, Vishnu, and Shiva…Swaha
93. Who is the embodiment of all riches…Swaha
94. Who is ever ready to protect all people…Swaha
95. Who is the celibate Goddess…Swaha
96. Who is the protectress of the Gods…Swaha
97. Who is the giver of all strength…Swaha
98. Who is the giver of ecstasy…Swaha
99. Who is awe inspiring…Swaha
100. Who is pure nectar…Swaha
101. Who is the source of desire…Swaha
102. Who wears the crown of glory…Swaha
103. Who is the ideal of nations…Swaha
104. Who is first amongst the brave…Swaha
105. Who drinks the nectar of the lotus…Swaha
106. Who blesses the whole world…Swaha
107. Who sends the light force…Swaha
108. Who graces the universe…Swaha

Awakening the Divine Mother Energy

Kundalini should be treated as the Mother Herself. I once asked Ida Rolf, the founder of Rolfing, about the meaning of kundalini. She said, "Oh, Sondra, only God understands that."

In the book, *Kundalini: The Secret of Life*, Muktananda says that the experience of kundalini is the true rebirth in which one is catapulted into a new world. He states that its unfolding has produced the great mystics and beings of genius in every age. In the chapter, "The Nature of Kundalini," Muktananda describes how every tradition speaks of kundalini in its own way: "In Japanese, it is called Ki; in Chinese, it is called Chi; in Christianity, it is called the Holy Spirit. Whatever it is called, it is the power of consciousness. It is supreme energy that the sages of India worship as the Divine Mother." He goes on to say that this energy can be awakened by intense devotion to God, through repetition of a mantra, through activation from a master, and through types of breathing meditations.

I feel lucky that my masters Babaji, Shastriji, Ammachi, and Jesus, as well as the breathing process itself awakened my kundalini. When the elements are purified enough in a person (such as through the Liberation Breathing® technique) the kundalini shakti has a free path to move through the chakras. It cleans you out! It is very good to know that you can be given a new life. Muktananda also said in *Kundalini: The Secret of Life*: "There is no such thing as giving it to one and denying it to another. If one asks to whom the sun gives heat the answer is to whoever stands in front of it."

Indian mystic Gopi Krishna, author of *Kundalini: The Evolutionary Energy in Man*, describes kundalini as "the supreme mistress of the body…the queen and architect of the living organism, having the power to mold, transform, or even to destroy it as she will." He notes that awakening of the kundalini is a regular theme in ancient hymns and signifies a change in the whole function of the cells, tissues, and brain, capable of opening transcendental knowledge and super-normal psychic powers.

I am convinced that adding the prayers and mantras of the Divine Mother to the breathing session makes it totally safe to let the kundalini rise!

A Scientific Explanation by Eve Jones

Over her lengthy career, clinical psychologist Dr. Eve Jones introduced thousands of health professionals to rebirthing through private sessions, writings, and lectures. Her specializations in neuropharmacology, endocrinology, physiology, and biology provide a unique window into the scientific nature of the work. Below are excerpts from her text *An Introduction to Rebirthing for Health Professionals* that detail some of the scientific aspects of Liberation Breathing®:

"Vitality or good health is related to the rate at which the body turns over energy in the anabolic and catabolic functions. The faster we make or repair or replace old body stuff, the healthier we are. The faster we eliminate wastes produced by such work, or by tissue breakdown, the more easily the body keeps itself in good order…Hypothetically, disease can be resisted and old age can be delayed or partially reversed by providing the body a sufficiency of the building blocks it uses, free of pollutants, and by maximizing the effectiveness with which the body eliminates waste.

"It's important to recognize the part played by simple respiration as means of eliminating wastes from the body. Surprisingly only 3 percent of total body wastes are eliminated via defecation and only 7 percent via urination. The skin passes out another 20 percent, leaving the remaining 70 percent to be breathed out. I am not disputing the importance of a high bulk diet and plenty of water or of working up a good sweat; I'm merely calling attention to the immense amount of work that breathing performs. It obviously behooves us to breathe fully and freely and to breathe clean air.

"Yet, when we investigate breathing, we find that most people aren't breathing most of the time! They tend to take their inhale as a short gasp which they hold for a while before exhaling in a long exhale and then they stay collapsed on the exhale for another long pause before starting the next gasp in. The amount of time they spend both inhaling and exhaling is shorter than the time they spend not doing either…Fortunately our breath is under our control partially and our body reliably alters heart rate as respiratory rate changes. So we can have the benefits of safely increasing heart rate, without producing new metabolites to labor our body with, simply by concentrating our consciousness on our breath and breathing fully…

"Since most people don't breathe consciously and in a connected manner most of the time, their breathing isn't used to heal most of the time. But the mechanism is there, ready to be revived and utilized whenever the person overcomes whatever unwillingness exists to using it. For that seems to be the central issue—the reason we don't breathe in the connected pattern constantly as contented animals appear to do and as people in deep sleep do, is that we cling to our attachment to emotionally charged reactions and we are afraid to give them up as we would do in the course of breathing consciously.

"To date, thousands of people who have become breathworkers have been involved in helping tens of thousands of people with significant physical problems including acne, alcoholism, angina, anorexia nervosa, arthritis, asthma, barbiturate addictions, bulimia, chronic bronchitis, diabetes, digestive disorders, epilepsy, hypertension, menstrual disorders, nicotine addiction, obesity, opiate addiction, poor peripheral circulation, post traumatic conditions, sexual disorders, spastic paralysis, tranquilizer addictions, upper respiratory disorders and more. Patients with allergies, cancers, duodenal ulcers, gastric ulcers, kidney problems, and migraines have been rebirthed successfully. In addition to this wide variety of physical ailments, every type of neurotic and psychotic personality disorder have been rebirthed successfully, and have made major personality changes for the better within a matter of a few sessions.

"In addition to providing for the material benefit of your patients by teaching them rebirthing techniques you may even be instrumental in promoting another source of ease and peace. It profoundly alters the relationship between the healed and the healer. I am totally confident that you will find it everything you ever dreamed of when you first considered taking care of others.

"In peace, simplicity and love. Breathe!"

—Dr. Eve Jones

Prana and Rejuvination—What the Mystics Say

The yogis of ancient India and other cultures have known for millennia the essential relationship between life and breath. They developed breathing practices to make contact with the Divine, with the very source of life itself. They called these practices *pranayama* in which the breath is controlled. By practicing pranayama the vibrational frequency of the mind and body rises to make contact with spirit.

Prana, or Life Force, is much more subtle than air alone. It is the very building block of life energy that permeates all things. Pranayama was designed to make direct contact with this life energy (not always accessible during regular breathing). Pranayama traditionally requires years of practice and dedication. The beauty of the Liberation Breathing® breath is that it connects you with prana, minus the restraint and arduous practice needed to perform the more traditional forms of pranayama. It is simply a deep and consciously connected circular breath, with no holding at the top and no holding at the bottom.

Baird Spalding, in the *Life and Teachings of the Masters of the Far East* writes about prana in the following way: "A Cosmic Life Force surrounds and interpenetrates every condition and atom. That life force can be drawn within our bodies along with the breath we breathe. But it is not the mere act of breathing that draws this cosmic life force into the body of man. Unless definite attention to it accompanies our physical breathing, it is not fully appropriated. This cosmic life force is sometimes called Prana. Prana is not oxygen, but rather is that which gives life to the oxygen, the actual life force within the oxygen" (Vol. 4, Chapter 12).

Spalding emphasizes that the mystics know how to realize the "inner breath" that links the outer attention to the inner attention, drawing the elements of the cosmic universe into man's universe through:
- an understanding that everything to which your attention is directed leaves an impression on the mind
- deep abiding attention to the surrounding spiritual ethers
- a completely relaxed body

- all-absorbing interest
- complete openness of mind
- nurturing the deep inner longing of acknowledging perfection within oneself and the universe

Applying this to Liberation Breathing®, one develops the idea of inner attention or "mental breathing" to consciously access the Cosmic Life Force. Liberation Breathing® is a form of pranic breathing. Prana, when breathed into the body in quietness and confidence, accesses every cell of the being and becomes the sustaining and invigorating element of life and the human body. This causes the body to keep young and vibrant. It allows the cells and tissue to expand and brings greater oxidation to the body. It is a complete "spiritual airing" of every cell.

Spalding notes that prana is called the Spirit of God in the scriptures. Pranayama is the art of spiritual breathing. This practice revitalizes the body and also enlivens the mind. With spiritual breathing, one's whole nature is expanded and functions more freely and completely. Memory comes in from a thousand different sources and one remembers what one was in the beginning. Anything one wants to know comes instantly and easily into the mind. Prana is one of the elements of Spirit. Spirit is not only energy but intelligence and substance. It is even more subtle than ether. Spirit is also that which cannot be destroyed. Prana is always active. There are those who overcome old age and death through an understanding of prana; they rebuild the body with pranic influence. This primal intelligence, life force, and substance are God in action.

When we go back to the center of anything, it is pure light. This is the inner light of which Jesus spoke. It is the light of illumination. The greater man's spiritual awakening, the greater the light is. When one lives in the light, one becomes immortal, for the light never dies. Pranic light can always be used to overcome degrading or conflicting forces. State the following:

I am the force of pranic light.
I project it and put it forth as all powerful.

Spiritual breathing (Liberation Breathing®) is receiving into the consciousness of man that which is within the spiritual ethers. Relaxed, quiet attention is the secret. As you breathe, your energy balance increases. You take in more and use less. This energy then opens up the body at all levels—physical, emotional, mental, and spiritual. Any points of resistance are cleared by this energy as it expands and increases in charge. Pranic breathing gives a wider view of life and frees the mind, which in turn frees the body. Give your whole being a good pranic airing and go into the light.

Visual Recall—A Session in Pictures

During a Liberation Breathing® session—possibly even the first session—you may recall your birth scene. Or, you may become so preoccupied with your physical body that you will care little about memories and pictures. I myself am not very visual, but rather auditory. Some people who are visual see lots of pictures and it is pretty exciting. The pictures may become more and more obvious with each subsequent session, and after you have worked out your physiological stuff, you can sit down quietly and recall events from your birth. In other words, after the trauma has been removed, you will have the tendency to gain full memory of your birth experience and the events surrounding it. This is extremely valuable because you will be able to see how this has been running your life.

I have given sessions to several people who were adopted and had no conscious recall of their natural parents prior to that day. In their experiences, they were literally able to "see" their natural mothers and fathers and give incredible details about why they were adopted which enabled them to forgive the parents for having given them up. *How do I explain this?* I don't know. Infinite Intelligence is there. Thousands of people have remembered details they were never told. These details were then checked out with the parents and confirmed, much to their amazement.

The main reason some people have trouble seeing or remembering their birth is that negative mental mass inhibits them from remembering anything before a certain age. A good affirmation to remove this memory block is, "My mind is immersed in Infinite Intelligence and can deliver information to me about my past, present, and future." Memory blocks caused by past traumatic experiences are a common subject of psychology. The theory is that painful experiences are blocked from memory because the person does not want to remember the pain.

Liberation Breathing® theory is that remembering the experience releases the pain and frees the mind and body, and that the release is not painful. The fear of painful memories holds the pain in the mind or body to be experienced as pain or tension. To free your memory you have to get rid of the concept that remembering painful incidents makes the pain worse; you have to get into the idea that the release is worth the time and it is wonderful. I can verify this absolutely in my experience.

Liberation Breathing® is focused on releasing trauma rather than indulging in it. Most people when taking out their household garbage don't examine each piece of garbage before they dump it. They just *dump* it. However, it is a curious phenomenon that those same people, before letting go of any psychological garbage, will find it necessary to meticulously pick through, sift, taste, touch, smell, analyze, and classify each item in order to make sure they don't throw out anything valuable. Liberation Breathing® is like carrying out your garbage in one fell swoop. In the beginning some people find this very disconcerting because the breathing process releases negative mental mass so quickly that you don't have time to think about it or understand it. Most people tell us that they got more out of one or two breathing sessions than many years of therapy.

In Liberation Breathing®, practitioners study a person's conception, prenatal experience, birth trauma, post-partum trauma, early childhood, and anything else in one's life that needs clearing.

Why Liberation Breathing Diverges from Other Practices

We consider Liberation Breathing® to be a spiritual purification technique. It is a medium for miracles, which are shifts in a person's overall perception. It is a process of complete *forgiveness*. The breather exerts the process on him or herself.

The practitioner coaches the breathing process, focuses the client, and helps the breather feel safe.

There are a few things Liberation Breathing® is not. It is not Primal Scream. We do not indulge in anger during the sessions, because any "anger" can be released on the exhale, while changing the thought that causes the anger. In extreme cases where a person has an intense need to feel the anger, we instruct them to do a scissors kick without bending the knees, while breathing vigorously and pumping out the anger with their exhale. Excessively indulging in expressing anger has been shown to damage a person's spiritual meridians. In our work we also teach everyone the consequences of anger, and help them to drop anger permanently. Anger is mostly an internal issue. External yelling and making sounds does not release the charge, we find, as much as the actual breathing and changing of the thoughts that are the root cause.

This does not mean that Liberation Breathing® suppresses emotion. Just the opposite. Emotions such as deep sadness and fear may come up, and we encourage people to work through these emotions. We often instruct breathers to "Inhale Love. Exhale fear." People carry around grief for years, and sometimes in one session their whole life changes as a result of releasing this long held sadness and intense remorse. All this happens very naturally. People "let up" what they are ready to release, and it is not the job of the practitioner to "induce" the breather into an artificial state of emotional catharsis. There are some breathworkers who do this, and we feel it is a violation of the integrity of the session and the sovereignty of the client.

In breathwork the client takes in the light through the breathing process, dispelling the darkness. It is as simple as "switching on the light." *A Course in Miracles* asks this of traditional psychotherapy: "Can you find light by analyzing darkness...?" (T9 V. 6:3) We have seen many psychotherapists and health practitioners add breathwork to their practices to get to the light and, thus, get extremely fast results.

In Liberation Breathing®, the breather is responsible for his own healing process. There is a natural equality between the breather and practitioner, who serves as a mirror for the client to see how his thoughts produce his results. No longer is the client a "victim" of past events "beyond his control." Rather, he begins to see that all past events are the results of his thoughts attracting his experiences. Thoughts always precede the experience. The practitioner's job is to help the client take 100 percent responsibility, which is the real catalyst for true change.

As we've mentioned, conscious, connected breathing works on its own, therefore we do not mix other modalities in with it. We want people to learn the power of their own breath; and if other techniques are mixed in, it dilutes this power and causes confusion. On occasion, rebirthing has been hybridized and combined with other practices. In some instances, those calling themselves "rebirthers" may have had limited training or even no association with the true practice of rebirthing/breathwork whatsoever. Over the past decade in the United States, two serious, separate incidences (resulting in deaths and criminal convictions of abuse) were referred to by the press as "rebirths" and the practitioners as "rebirthers" when, in fact, the abusive practices had absolutely no connection to rebirthing and conscious, connected breathing. This is a disservice to all the excellent breathworkers around the world who are doing great work. Many, many miracles have occurred with professional rebirthers. We support rebirthing totally when done by well-trained rebirthing breathwork and Liberation Breathing® practitioners.

Liberation Breathing in a Group or Seminar

In seminars and long-term programs we often practice Liberation Breathing® in a group, assisted by a team of qualified LB® practitioners. Liberation Breathing® in a group is not a replacement for private sessions, but has its own outstanding benefits. During Liberation Breathing® seminars people are asked to look at very deep, internal patterns and issues. They are presented with new philosophies of life that stretch their old belief systems. Therefore, it is useful for students to breathe through these changes, which helps integrate new thoughts and let go of negativity stuck in the mind and body. It is important that people in a seminar don't sit in their chairs with all the discomforts they might be holding in their bodies. For this reason people love to lie down and breathe. We often play Divine Mother chants to lift the energy higher, and it's very safe because the Divine Mother and the Divine Father are constantly present.

We find that a group Liberation Breathing® session at the end of each seminar day is an excellent completion. People find it uplifting and often have an insight of clarity and a vision of their own inner joy and sacredness. Group breathing sessions also bring up memories of the nursery for some, according to their particular birth script. When students breathe together it brings more energy into the room. Some even have visions of Holy beings. The participants become closer to each other, the sharing at the end becomes intimate, and everyone learns from one another during each session.

Recently, one of my dreams for Liberation Breathing® came true. I have always wanted to facilitate a group breathing session for an entire church because my own church dogma left me confused and mixed up, as it has done with many of my clients. I got the miracle I longed for when Reverend Cherie Larkin at Unity of Nashville in Nashville, TN, asked her church to sponsor me. Not only did she invite me to give a morning sermon, but she also sponsored one of my all-day seminars on the *New Frequency of Relationships*.

At the end of each seminar I always lead a group Liberation Breathing® session. In this instance, we had 75 people who had never experienced a breathing session before—a rare occurrence. Believe it or not, we actually had them all lie down in the church pews (which fortunately were padded) with their heads facing the aisles. The minister laid right down with them. My team and I were in awe of this. It was historical for us—a real first. Afterwards they shared of countless miracles and were in ecstasy.

Part 2

The Experience of Liberation Breathing

Ricardo's First Liberation Breathing Experience

Markus and I were not only thrilled about this session, we were astonished, as it happened to be our client's first Liberation Breathing® session with us. His life was forever changed in 90 minutes. He was so moved that he and his wife followed us to India where they went all the way. They became the purist of the pure. You can see the joy on their shining faces. This is Ricardo's account of his experience:

"I experienced the most important episode of my life in my Liberation Breathing private session with Sondra Ray and Markus. I went to this session without great expectations, only with the desire to go deeper in my experiences and learn more about how people who are advanced in this practice are working with Liberation Breathing. At the beginning of the session they asked me many questions about my birth, relationship with parents, and childhood. They asked me if there was something specific that I would like to work on in that session. I said that I had been practicing rebirthing breathwork for a few months, and that my experiences were pretty tranquil, linear and repetitive. I sincerely wanted to understand why this was happening. Was it because I really didn't have any deep inner issues to be worked out? Or, was it because I had strong blocks that I was not ready to release? They asked me to start breathing and we would find out. At this point I had already reported that I was born from a very long cesarean birth. My mother was hospitalized on Saturday and I was born on Monday. My family was very worried about the delay and also with the fact that a healer said my birth was under the influence of a curse from an old girlfriend of my father. I began to breathe normally, and they were going deeper into my personal lie, which at the time was: 'I am not able.' Sometimes I repeated affirmative sentences about my ability while I was breathing.

"At one point they put on the sound of the Aarti, a Sanskrit chant honoring Babaji, and suddenly I started to get into a state of total ecstasy, happiness, love, contentment, plenitude, gratitude and completeness. It's hard to put into words a feeling so strong and vivid. I started with slight smiles, the heart getting warm with so much love, and suddenly I was compulsively crying, shouting out with an inner feeling of happiness and gratitude for life. I could feel all my cells, my body vibrating as if I was totally plugged into an electrical grid, receiving a shock of thousands of volts. I raised my arms and thus received more energy. It felt and looked like something from heaven came inside of me through my hands. I followed my intuition in body movements and observed this energy as star-shaped, feeling the expansion of my body with such energy. I gave my hands to Sondra, Markus and Shubha (the gentle translator who accompanied us) willing to share and show them all of what I was feeling. Sometimes I shouted, 'It's beautiful,' 'Love,' 'Thank you,' 'I forgive you,' and said I did not want to leave that plenitude. To bring this energy to humanity was what I wanted most.

"Sondra asked me if I was seeing Babaji but I did not see Him, and did not need to see, because I was *feeling* the fullness of the Universe within me and it is superior to any vision. I let go completely. It seems that I freed and liberated everything that was inside me. I surrendered entirely to that experience, living a love I never experienced before. Whenever Sondra Ray spoke about Babaji and India my heart warmed and I could not hold back the tears and screams of delight that were coming straight from my heart. This experience was totally conscious. I felt no fear, nor hesitation at any time.

"It looked like I was in touch with God. If I died at that moment there would be no problem because I had just experienced the presence of God within me. It was very strong, words simply cannot match the moment. At first I had decided not to talk about the experience with the fear of not having the right words for something so special. After, I felt I needed to share it with my friends. Sondra Ray said that it was the true liberation and rebirth. At the end of the session I called my wife, asking her to meet me at the hotel because I wanted to share it with all that energy. After the session, when I arrived in the lobby of the hotel, I felt as if I was floating. I hugged my wife and at that moment she could also feel the energy of love that consumed me completely inside. I could only tell her the whole experience throughout the day, gradually, because the vibration was so strong that I just could not speak without starting to cry and live it all over again.

"When I arrived at work, I found a fellow who looked at me and immediately said she felt like crying. The last time she cried was at the death of her father (10 years prior). Another colleague looked at me, all day, saying that I looked like I had received a shock. He was right. When I shared the experience with friends, they were thrilled. Many cried and also could not put into words why they had this feeling. Even when I reported it to a friend by email, he told me he was all but vibrating inside while reading my email. It was a beautiful experience. I felt a certain 'pain' in the region of the heart for a few days. Over the weeks I was feeling kind of strange, something I still do not know how to explain, something that was not yet integrated. It looks like I was living as an old Ricardo along with a new Ricardo in the same body.

"I felt many details of my personal lie going away, especially when I started preparing for the trip to India. In former times, my personal lie (I'm not able) would stop me from living this experience. I would put a thousand obstacles, excuses, limitations and fears in the way. This time, none of that happened. I had less than one month and a half to arrange our passports, visa, money and everything else that was required to participate in India Quest. Everything worked well and far ahead of the date scheduled. I think I was completely in tune with life, with my life's purpose.

"We went to India and experienced many days of intense presence and plenitude, participated in the ritual Mundum (shaving off the hair) in the River Ganges, and I offered to the river the *old* Ricardo along with the hair that was shaved. I offered that part of us that needs to die so the new can be born, grow, evolve, transcend and illuminate the lives of others. At the end of this great existential adventure, I left those mountains in tears. I think it was the first time that my soul cried. I am in total gratitude for Liberation Breathing, Babaji and the Divine Mother, the India Quest, and Sondra and Markus who helped me to make these important inner transformations."

—Ricardo Queiroz Alexandre,
Belo Horizonte, Brasil

Ricardo and Maria took their experience of Liberation Breathing® one step further to immerse themselves in the India Quest. Since Babaji and the Divine Mother are the head and body of Liberation Breathing®, a trip to Haidakhan during the Spring Navaratri (Divine Mother Festival) is the highest thing we can offer. The sacred head shaving ceremony (Mundun) is totally optional. Some decide to take this step of inner transformation in addition to their Liberation Breathing® practice and experience.

Markus and Madame Pele On the Big Island of Hawaii

On the edge of Kilauea, I see the crater in the crater, Halema'uma'u, the home of Madame Pele, the Goddess of Fire and Volcanoes in the Hawaiian pantheon. Up from the depths of the earth the molten lava brews. Gasses of hot air spew forth from the many scattered fissures and the large vent deep in the crater. From the floor of Pele's home, a cloud of gasses ascends into the atmosphere, forming a huge white plume of smoke that rises into the sky and travels across the firmament. The vastness of the Caldera brings my mind to stillness. As I stand on its edge, I am spooked a little that the drop to the floor of the crater is over five hundred feet below. It is an awesome sight. I breathe in appreciation for this sacred place of natural power and beauty. A sense of deep gratitude comes over me.

Our Hawaiian guide and teacher gives our group of students an overview of the ancient lore, and invites us to go into our own personal meditation close to the crater's edge. He begins to chant some ancient Hawaiian invocations. Beautiful and sonorously fresh, the sounds of his voice transport us into a meditative state of inner calm. We listen to the melodious chant as he projects his words out over the vast space above the crater. I feel the collective power of our group as we focus our minds to bring in the attention of the Goddess. We pay Her homage as She gives us the boon of Her communion.

As the Kahuna stops his chanting, a profound silence comes over me. Gently, I flatten myself out on the cinder-covered ground and make a little pillow under my head with my wallet. Resting on the rocky surface, the breath of Pele begins to flow into me. I take Her into my lungs. Liberation Breathing® with the Divine Mother is something that comes directly into you. The freshness of the early morning atmosphere cleanses me of my thoughts and concerns. It is time to let go and be in the moment of Divine perfection. I breathe deeply and smoothly, grateful to be present at one of the most sacred spots on Earth, at the place where the Mother forms Herself from the fire of molten rock. One final chant goes out over the crater, an expression of our thanks to the Goddess for hearing our prayers of gratitude. As time stops, I feel the presence of the Divine Mother everywhere.

I walk in silence with the stillness of an inner peace enveloping my whole being, holding the hand of my mate, afresh with a renewed gratitude for Liberation Breathing®. It came to me so effortlessly, without asking, lying on the ancient ground at the edge of Madame Pele's home. A fire of Divine grace infuses into the very breath and blood that sustains my existence from the Mother Herself, charging me up for yet another year. We come annually to visit Halema'uma'u, the home of the Fire Goddess, where all the forces of Pele are at our disposal. They infuse us with the inspiration to be Her representatives as we travel around the world teaching people the life-enhancing and liberating qualities of Her breath. I am in an altered state of intense gratitude. We let the energy of the past hour soak in and cover us with the palpable blessing of this encounter. We are all in the embrace of the Divine Mother.

Markus Chronicles A Liberation Breathing Intensive in Australia

Hitting ground in Brisbane, Australia, we are delighted to be back to this land of inherently positive people with "no worries, Mate." We exit the baggage claim and look around the terminal for our organizer, Brad Strickland, to appear. He is a farmer who sold his spread to move to the coast and start a Babaji Center in the mountains just west of the Gold Coast. After connecting with hugs and loading the car, we leave the coastal cities for the woods. Soon the land becomes green and pastoral as we head into the high ground of the mountains. The vistas are spectacular. Driving through this land so green and productive makes us feel safe and well cared for as we wind along the ascending switchbacks of the narrow local roads. The eucalyptus groves line the sides of the highway, producing a canopy of green cathedral-like foliage. By and by we arrive at Brad's "Mountain of Eden" estate. A series of small bungalows with Balinese grass roofs line the driveway—cozy little cottages with hot tubs for wet breathwork. We get our rest for the night and head out early the next morning for the site of the seminar.

In the meeting hall, we set up an altar with pictures of our spiritual masters along with flowers honoring them. This is the first thing we do in any seminar to honor the Divine Forces and Teachers who make our work possible. There are ten students attending the Liberation Breathing® Intensive. Most have had prior breathwork experience, but two have had none—a bold move. We get acquainted and invite each person to introduce themselves by telling us what they know about their birth scripts. Everyone has a unique story, and I take notes on an index card for each as their stories unfold. I also take notes on their "personal lie" that we discuss later, and any other negative thoughts they may share with the group. Usually people reveal what is not working in their life; one just has to be a good listener. These are the very thoughts that need to be reversed. Listening to people's stories is something we do well. Together, Sondra and I are like Sherlock Holmes for the mind. We trace back the students' negative thoughts. Liberation from these thoughts is the main purpose of Liberation Breathing®.

After lunch the group is well bonded, and we pair students up for Liberation Breathing®. Some people go into the drama of unresolved past experiences. Our Danish student and chef for the group has unresolved anger and resentment towards his father for not being there for him. The *parental disapproval syndrome* is a major portion of our psyche that needs to be cleared. He goes into a lot of shouting in his breathing session, which we discourage. Expressing anger does not mean it is being released. It is better to get in touch with the sadness underlying the anger, and then take responsibility for the experience through forgiveness.

After an hour of breathing, student pairs switch from breather to practitioner. Sondra and I circulate and help the newer students with their breathing sessions. As students breathe, we ask, "What is coming up in your mind?" If they are having a physical symptom, we ask, "What thought is behind your symptom?"

Liberation Breathing® is designed to pull these thoughts out of us, so we can be free of their effects. We "extract" thoughts that produce problems in life—both immediate and long range. Without a pre-existing thought, a problem cannot happen. It is like a program on a CD or hard drive: remove the CD and it cannot play. Delete, delete, delete. Most of the process of Liberation Breathing® is one of undoing and removing negative thought forms and then accepting the power of your own being in the present. Breath is an essential action of life, and our function in life is to achieve pure joy.

On the mountain roads back to the seminar the next morning the rain persists from the day before. The fields are an intense green. Fertility is all around us as Australia is in the middle of its spring. The pastures are full of cows with newborn calves suckling. In the lowlands, the countryside scenes resemble a John Constable painting. Trees and small brooks spread across the land. Rolling hills rise up and take our breath away with their natural beauty. We roll into the retreat center as our group is having a lively breakfast. We share some coffee with students and then head down the concrete walkway through the lush vegetation toward the meeting hall.

The day is spent discussing how the type of birth we had affects our life and relationships. This material is fascinating, as people are startled and intrigued that they were fully conscious beings at the time of their birth. This section on birth and relationships has everyone on the edge of their chairs. Everyone wants to know how they came into this life and how that affects them. Sondra is an expert in this area, having studied it and written a number of books on the subject. The people in the training know and appreciate this.

The students look at these factors in their breathing session in the afternoon. I am always amazed at how my own inducement at birth makes me feel somewhat manipulated to be in situations I am not ready for…when in fact I was actually overdeveloped (24" at birth and 9 lbs. 10 oz. in weight) and *more* than ready! It took me over two years to accept the fact I was supposed to be up front with Sondra teaching the classes. I found all kinds of ways to hide out in the "womb" and not come forth into my power.

After the sessions of breathing we all gather in the cozy lounge area for dinner. The Danish chef has produced a lovely spread, and we all cap off the day with a meal together. The bond between us is getting closer, and I can feel people loosening up and letting down their defenses. Soon after dinner we head back to Brad's place. Of course, it is still raining.

The next morning we join the students for breakfast. Soon after we resume our lectures on the dynamics of family patterns. Most of us see how our relationship with our parents and siblings had a huge impact on the quality of our relationships. Sondra's Loving Relationship Training® is one of the best seminars for looking at these inherited family patterns, and we present a major portion of this information in the LBI in Australia. People are reeling from the realization that they have recreated situations and patterns in their lives due to the conditioning of the family. As teachers we often receive new insights into the depths of how these patterns affect our life and relationships right now.

The afternoon breathe is more powerful than the day before. One young woman goes into tetany, a stiffness in the hands that comes when breathing is forced or blocked with some negative thought held in the subconscious. We ask her, "What is the negative thought stuck in your hands?" "I can't let go," is the answer. "Of what?" we ask. "I'm not good enough…and I don't want to be here!" comes the answer. Those are the thoughts stuck in her hands. So now we give her a different thought that expresses her Higher Self: "Because I accept I am good enough, I want to be here to express my joy." She recites this thought back to us. Within minutes the stiffness in her hands subsides. For her the miracle is seeing the thought "I am not good enough" has been sabotaging her life, and the thought "I *am* good enough" has all the potential to transform it.

By now we are one big happy family, and people are opening up not only in the sessions but at the meals as well. Our Danish chef is beginning to see his case with his dad is "up." He became a rebel and left the country, traveling all over the world working on organic farms, but a nagging feeling inside makes him angry. His most negative thought about himself—that he is bad—formed as a result of a heavy dose of parental disapproval from his dad. The giving nature he has most of the time becomes sabotaged by this thought, and it turns people away. He gives through the food, but his conversation is often tinged with an edge of irritation and smugness. We know we have to work with him in the breathing sessions on this issue, because it is holding him back in life.

The energy intensifies in the session room. On the fourth day we discover we can light a fire in the wood burning stove, so we stoke it up. The rain has been falling for days and it seems it is never letting up…so the fire is just what we all need to warm up our inner heat. We recite the 108 Divine Mother names before each class in the morning. "Om, I bow to her the Mother of Fire…Swaha!" Thank goodness She warms us up with fire! On this fourth day people are really getting into honoring the Divine Mother. We would not have physical existence without Her. We could not take a breath without Her. The sessions that afternoon are very powerful. One of the ladies from Wagga Wagga who is there with her husband has an intense rush of energy move through her body. She shakes for about a minute and then comes to a complete catharsis of her case. Gratitude sweeps over her and we are so grateful Liberation Breathing® is moving her into a transformed state of being.

That evening at dinner her husband tells us this is the best training on breathwork he has ever done…and he has had a lot of training. One program he did lasted a whole year. He said the gentleness and directness of Liberation Breathing® far surpasses the effectiveness of much more invasive and emotionally engaging forms of breathwork he has been taught. Yes! We have a saying at the LB® Intensive: "Drama does not release trauma." People are given space to find their own balance within. Feelings come up to release from one's system, not to hang onto and dramatize.

Our Danish student is still activated in anger about his father, and he acts it out in his session with some screaming. We encourage him to give up the drama and come to forgiveness of his father. Also, he needs to own his part in attracting that father in this lifetime for certain lessons on which he was incomplete before this incarnation. He is slow to give up his anger. I notice I am getting tired of the same "record playing." I gently suggest to him that he is stealing the attention of the group with this ranting of his anger in the session, which he has done for four days now. He needs to take responsibility for giving it up, and contain himself now.

That evening at the dinner there is a warm and welcome feeling of community. Four of the young women from Sydney agree to produce a Loving Relationships Training® next year. A woman from Byron Bay agrees to help our organizer, Brad, with another Liberation Breathing Intensive in the Gold Coast area. The couple from Wagga Wagga commits to coming with us on India Quest for the Divine Mother festival. All is flowing and clearing in the most miraculous way.

On the final day we complete with a group Liberation Breathing® session, as we play the immortality chant through the whole breathe. Another fire is roaring in the stove. Before the last session we assess each student individually with our feedback from the whole training, which we have written up on a page with affirmations and recommendations. Everyone hears this feedback with the utmost respect…and all agree with these completions. The energy in the room is one of extreme gratitude by the time we breathe. People feel liberated from their past. And as we all lay down to breathe in the presence of the Divine Mother, who has blessed our retreat with Her Grace, our Danish friend smiles in a beaming face of true transformation…and goes the whole session without one outburst of drama or anger. *Om Namah Shivay!*

An Obstetrician Discovers Birth-Day Consciousness

The following essay by Dr. Robert P. Doughton chronicles the shifts and shocks that occur when the strongholds of one's professional life are uprooted by the gift of conscious, connected breathing:

"In 1976, a young man stayed overnight at my house as part of a weekend seminar in which we were both participants. His name was Ned Jastram. He was totally fascinated by the fact that at that time I made much of my living by 'delivering babies.' He asked me if I was aware that children in the womb were conscious and remembered their birth. I was completely clear that their memory was not yet developed, and that their consciousness was minimal beyond sleep and hunger. My answer was, 'Of course they do not.'

"In defense of my ignorance, I did see at once that if what Ned said was true, then my world would be rocked, and probably for the good. I simply did not believe him. In every other way Ned seemed a responsible and reliable citizen, his father was a physicist and rather well known in New England. He was not in rebellion against his parents; he was in school and a good student and related to me and others in a friendly manner.

"I asked him how he learned to do this retrieval of this memory of birth. He told me that he learned the technique from Leonard Orr who discovered it. I told him that I would submit to this breathing process, pay him money, and see what transpired.

"Five rebirthing sessions later I was present in my mother's birth canal, interacting with her and the doctor. I found myself fully conscious, telling him how to deliver my arm so that it would be easy. I saw my father in the room looking 30 years old. I was aware of the doctor and his consciousness and assessed him as a true gentleman. I was aware of the nurse and fascinated by her breasts as something I should definitely check out. I was focused on the shiny silvery chrome top of a sterilizer jar for cotton balls and did not want to quit looking at it. I saw my mom at age 29. I was thrilled to be born; my mother was equally thrilled; my father was simply alive with joy. The doctor and nurse were radiantly happy.

"This was life changing to me because, at age 43, I realized that my father and I had not been thrilled together since I was about three years old…far from it. The next time I saw my dad, I told him that I had 'snooped in' on my birth and was present to his thrill and joy of that moment. I recommended that from now on we focus more on that thrill than our differences. From that time on, he and I became best friends, lasting until his death 20 years later.

"This led me to change my medical practice so that most of my patients who were interested experienced their own birth prior to giving birth. I have now had the extreme pleasure to facilitate breathing sessions with about 15 children whom I 'delivered' in days gone by. They gave me their perceptions of me at that time (sometimes slightly embarrassing) as they could tell I was bored, excited, enthusiastic, brilliant, and the like. It helped to heal one baby whom we had to use mid forceps that hurt his head. In his session, he wanted permission to hit me back! I told him it was okay as long as it was symbolic only; he had to promise to not hurt me as much as the forceps hurt him. He and I are buddies today.

"I now know that 70 percent of one's life is influenced by what happens at birth, and I now know that this includes diseases, health problems, and the way you will think about experiences that will occur for you. In these few hours the ego, the defense mechanism, is formed and it influences huge parts of the rest of your life, yet our society largely ignores this fundamental true fact causing huge disadvantage to our personhood and our society.

"Because of Sondra Ray and Leonard Orr and their pioneering, I now know this and can myself teach it. When one is in possession of a truth so powerful as this—so counterintuitive from all of our society's teaching and orientation—one is almost in shock to know how to present this to an ordinary public, and humbled by the responsibility of how this transfer of knowledge can be accomplished, indeed transferred to where it will make the most difference. I thank God that Sondra and Leonard at one time pushed forward at their own personal expense at something so unreasonable, and after decades it is now going mainstream. It really has helped me in my life and career."

—Robert P. Doughton, M.D.,
American Board of Obstetrics and Gynecology

Part 3

Historical Landmarks of Liberation Breathing

My Path as a Healer

As a Nurse, MPH, and Nurse Practitioner with 14 years of experience, I became well equipped to speak on the subject of healing. Yet, as a practicing nurse I felt that I was often in the wrong end of medicine. I was trying to heal people *after* they had developed disease. *How did I know that after my patients went home and stopped the pills, they would not return?* Often, patients *did* come back with the same condition. *Where was permanent healing?* I realized I wanted to *prevent* people from getting sick and going into the hospital in the first place. This became my new mission. I was so excited. I felt totally committed to it because in rebirthing I saw people being healed permanently by breathing and changing their thoughts. I had another mission—and I *knew* it.

I was very fortunate that my final experiences as a nurse were in the area of prenatal nursing. I felt I was most productive teaching new mothers how to have healthier babies. In 1974, when Leonard Orr tried rebirthing on me, I became absolutely fascinated by the effects of birth trauma, and how one's thoughts affect the body. When Leonard convinced me that all pain was the effort involved in clinging to a negative thought, and that negative thoughts could be changed and breathed out, I knew for sure *that was it*. I gave up medicine altogether to study spiritual healing.

Rebirthing became my passion, my mission, my constant research, and my life. Previously, I'd never seen anything that produced permanent healing before my very eyes—in myself and in others. I had had a pain in my body for 15 years (which started when my father died). I tried everything in medicine and psychiatry to get rid of this pain, but nothing worked. The pain disappeared forever after only three rebirthing sessions! You can imagine my relief and joy. Today, I can unequivocally say that I have never seen anything heal a body like conscious, connected breathing.

Of course, it is perfectly fine to get help from the medical profession, just as I have done at various points. I have learned that doctors *are* God. And, we need to honor our own fears. Sometimes the fear of self-healing is so great you need medical help. It may take some time to learn self-healing. Liberation Breathing® is a good place to start.

The Loving Relationships Training

About a year after I started my practice as a rebirther, I noticed an amazing thing. Clients would come to me and tell me all about their relationships, their marriages, and their sex problems. I would rebirth them and they would have a birth memory. At that moment, I was suddenly able to see how their birth trauma was affecting their relationships! It was like light bulbs—I could see the connection so clearly.

I began to research how one's birth affects one's relationships. I kept it all quiet because it was something new and different, and I did not want to talk about it until the right time. One day Leonard came home and said, "They want you in Hawaii and I told them you were coming." I thought it was unusual he did not even ask me first, but every time I had this thought, I would do it anyway and miracles would happen.

I went to Hawaii. *How could I resist?* When I arrived, there were 25 people sitting on the floor waiting for me. I said, "Let me tell you what I have learned about how your birth affects your relationships." The day flew by and at the end they all sat there with their mouths hanging open staring at me. No one moved. Then, they started to say, "Sondra, this explains everything!" I had no idea of the power of this material or the impact it would make. They asked me to stay an extra day, as they wanted their friends to hear me talk. Their friends had the same exact reaction. They added that this was too much to integrate in one day and that I should write it up in a two-day outline. When I returned to San Francisco I wrote the first Loving Relationships Training®, known as the LRT®. News of the seminar travelled around the rebirthing community and suddenly I was invited everywhere. It was widely successful and we always led it in twos (both trainers being rebirthers). The training is now in its fourth decade around the world. I am proud of the LRT® because the curriculum can save people decades of time in learning how to handle relationships.

Frederick LeBoyer: Birth Without Violence

In 1975, I happened to read an article in *Vogue* about French obstetrician Dr. Frederick LeBoyer who was delivering babies using a method called *quiet birth*. He turned the lights low, helped the baby out gently, laid the newborn on the mother, and then placed the baby in warm water, with a delay of cord cutting. He wrote a very powerful book called *Birth without Violence*. It was so amazing that I suggested we have the client read from it aloud before going into water for wet breathing. I theorized that this would activate the birth trauma more, thus deepening the process. In our first trial, we placed the client on the couch between us and I instructed him to read certain pages out loud:

> This is the Golden Age.
> But it doesn't last.
> In the depths of the womb, the infant has been overtaken by Natural Law…
> One day labor starts. The delivery has begun.
> An intransigent force—wild, out of control—has gripped the infant.
> A blind force that hammers at it and impels it downward.
> It is no longer enough for the infant to bend its back.
> Overpowered, it huddles up as tightly as it can. With its head tucked in and its shoulders hunched together, it is hardly more than a little ball of fright.
> The prison has gone berserk, demanding its prisoner's death. The walls close in still further. The cell becomes a passageway; the passage, a tunnel.
> With its heart bursting, the infant sinks into this hell.
> Its fear is without limit.

While reading the passage aloud, our client became so activated that he went right into his birth trauma on the couch! He felt tingling all over, cried, and spontaneously breathed to the point that we did not even have time to get him into the water. We were amazed that someone could actually remember his birth without the experience of being in water. This was a revelation for us and it was the beginning of dry rebirthing in the world. We discovered that it was not so much the water that caused the memory of birth, but a certain type of breathing in the presence of someone who had already released his or her birth trauma. Their presence was somewhat like a vacuum cleaner. Telepathically it created the space for the other to feel safe enough to let it up. What this meant for us is that we could now travel around the world and spread rebirthing without always having to find a hot tub. People could simply lie down on a bed or a mat on the floor to breathe. It changed everything. Rebirthing spread like wild fire to many places and many countries.

At one early point, LeBoyer's book *Birth Without Violence* was even used to resolve an inquiry from Hawaii law enforcement! In Hawaii, small Japanese soaking tubs called furos were common, but it was difficult to find large hot tubs for wet breathing. The only hot tub I could locate was a demonstration model in a warehouse. The owner granted us after-hours access to the warehouse, and I took a group of eight eager persons for wet breathing, which went on into the night.

Everyone was lying around in bliss when I rebirthed the last person. She let out a yell and someone called the police. At her birth, she was delivered in a teaching hospital and had five males present including residents and medical students. *Guess how many cops came to the door?* Five! They walked in and saw her in the middle of her process and they could not figure out why the others showed no concern. They decided we were all on drugs so they searched the place. I went right on with my client and I told them to go ahead, as all they were going to find was guava juice.

The officers still thought the experience was strange, so I told my assistant to get LeBoyer's book *Birth without Violence*, which is filled with photos. She took them outside and carefully explained what we were doing through the illustrations in the book. One of the men understood and asked, "Do you have discounts for cops?" After discovering dry breathing, those wild days happened less frequently.

LeBoyer and the Rebirthing Movement Influence Obstetricians

Over the years we have had the pleasure of introducing rebirthing and Liberation Breathing® to many obstetricians, health care workers, and birthworkers. They, too, are pioneers working to improve the conditions for future generations of the world. Dr. Phil Dubois was one such obstetrician who trained and practiced in a conventional Midwestern medical center. The influence of gentle birth practices coupled with his own rebirthing experiences eventually led to a complete transformation within his obstetrics practice. Dubois describes his professional evolution in the following way:

"Birth for me was a crisis of survival and an interruption of my work schedule. I was tense all the way through labors and deliveries, wondering if something bad was going to happen or if I was going to have to do something drastic. At times I felt uncomfortable and distanced from the laboring woman and her partner. It seemed I was supposed to be able to do something that I didn't know how to do. I felt that I should be able to make the labor smooth and easy and the birth effortless and joyful. I wanted to, but it was not that way at all. Birth was the ultimate crisis for everybody. The parents, nurses, the baby and I would all be in a state of more or less controlled panic. The mother would scream in agony or be pathetically disconnected from the experience by sedation or anesthesia. The father would desperately try to comfort his mate or angrily demand something be done, or remain in a withdrawn state of helpless apathy. The nurses and I exerted tremendous effort to control our own upset while going through the ritual of plugging the mother into IVs, anesthetics, monitors, sterile preps, sterile drapes, and standard positioning in the stirrups.

"The baby was treated with all the respect and concern that any heart-lung preparation in an animal research lab would get. Every conceivable procedure was done to insure that those lungs would fill with air and that the heart would pump good blood through the warm flesh. This soul would be quickly separated from the placenta, taken to a table under bright lights, vigorously dried and stimulated, usually by flicking the bottom of its feet, tightly wrapped in a bulky blanket, briefly shown to or held by the mother, then whisked off to the nursery where it was weighed, stabbed with a shot, its eyes inoculated with a burning silver nitrate solution, a thermometer shoved up its rectum, measurements taken. Then it was left alone for several hours except for a watchful eye across the room.

"Then I saw Dr. LeBoyer on television, along with his film about gentle, loving birth. Parents began asking me for that kind of birth. I did not want to do it, but I finally agreed. The first birth I attended with the lights turned down was reassuring. After a few more tries, I began to notice that the mood in the delivery room was more calm and serene. The focus of attention was now on the baby and parents instead of instruments. I discovered that there was a person inside of that baby—a conscious, aware being who actually responded to my attention and caring. I was moved. My whole outlook on birth took a 180-degree turn. I looked forward to the joy and excitement of being there when a new person emerged into the world.

"*Then a friend of mine told me about rebirthing*. I finally went for it. I now know what bliss is all about. I sailed into the highest high I had ever experienced and it was easy. Since that time, I have been rebirthed several times and each one has been a profound experience for me. I now have a feeling of connection with the newborns. I know from my memories of my own birth, that recognition of the person inside the baby is what the baby needs more than anything else. Having worked through my own birth allows me to be there with the baby without getting plugged into my own birth memories. I talk to the baby at the moment of birth. I say, 'Hi, welcome to the world. It is a beautiful world.'"

—Dr. Phil Dubois

Meeting Babaji

In 1977, Leonard Orr and Sondra Ray were called to India by Babaji. The calling came in the form of an unusual letter sent to the Theta House in San Francisco with only three words: "Come to India." It was high time that Westerners arrived in Haidakhan to begin their own respective missions of Divine Service. It took two trips to India and about eight months to find Babaji. That Leonard and Sondra had already cleared major pieces of their birth trauma and death urge was a good thing, because Babaji wasted no time in smashing the remainder of their personal "issues" that may have stood in the way of their work as teachers in the West.

As told in Yogananda's *Autobiography of a Yogi*, Lahiri Mahasaya received the instruction of Kriya Yoga from Babaji in 1861 near Ranikhet in Northern India (the current site of Babaji's ashram of Chilianaula). This ancient form of meditation continues to be taught today through the lineage of Yogananda's Self-Realization Fellowship. When Leonard Orr and Sondra Ray met at the feet of Babaji in Haidakhan in 1977, He told them, "Rebirthing is the new Kriya Yoga. Westerners do not have the time for long meditations. This simplified form is what is needed in these fast-paced times." Thus, it was through Leonard and Sondra that two of Babaji's highest teachings—*conscious, connected breathing* and *physical immortality*—were transmitted. It is through them these wonderful teachings have spread worldwide.

To the degree that Babaji is the original Source of the remarkable process of rebirthing as channeled through Leonard Orr, the Divine Mother is the original source of Liberation Breathing® as channeled through Sondra Ray. They are the male and female counterparts that form the balance of this Divine manifestation. When Babaji took conscious departure in 1984, his parting words were: "I leave everything in the hands of the Divine Mother." As if on cue Sondra Ray's mission really began. Already she had created the Loving Relationships Training® that was being presented worldwide. Already she had left her lucrative career as a nurse practitioner to become a full time rebirther. Already she had published some of her major books on rebirthing, i.e., *Rebirthing in the New Age* with

Leonard Orr, *Birth and Relationships* with Bob Mandel, and *Ideal Birth*. Already she was becoming a well-respected voice in the self-help spiritual community in the United States.

After Babaji's conscious departure (called Samadhi), Sondra began taking groups of students to the Divine Mother Festival, or Navaratri, in India at Babaji's ashram every year. Thousands have been introduced to Babaji and the Divine Mother as a result of Sondra's unwavering dedication to her Master Haidakhan Babaji. Through His original inspiration, Babaji's influence is essential to Liberation Breathing®.

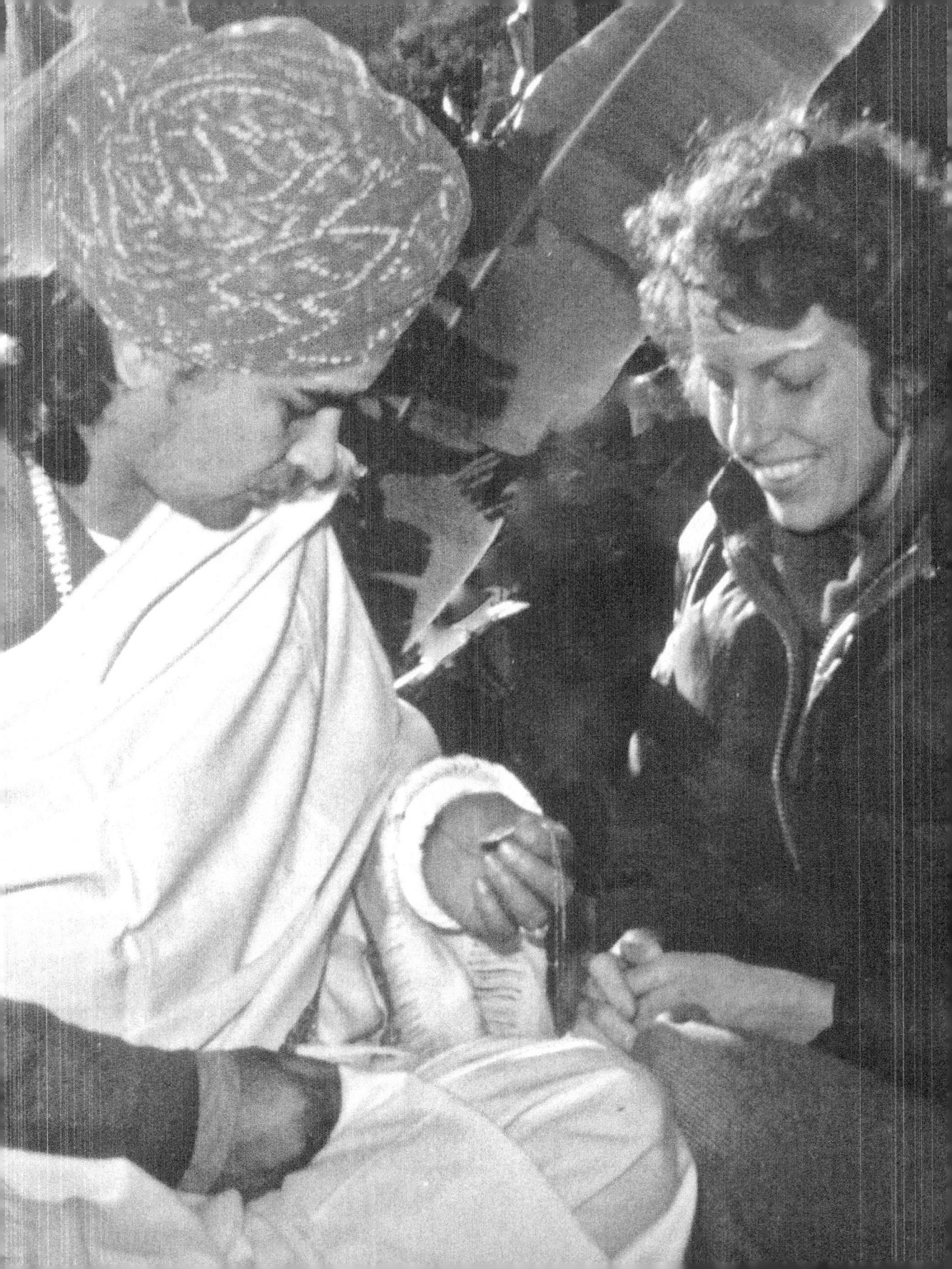

Rebirthing and Waterbirth in Russia

For some time, I wanted to go to Russia to meet waterbirth pioneer Igor Charkovsky. In the early 1980s, I smuggled my manuscript *Ideal Birth* through Sweden to him. Russia was a hard assignment because the Iron Curtain was still in place. I waited a long time to find the right moment to go. That moment happened when I met Rama Vernon who was a citizen diplomat. I felt safe going with her as she had made the trip many times.

My team of practitioners and I went through a lot crossing the border. The KGB ripped up the floors of our cabins. For the most part, they left me alone because I set up an altar to my guru, Babaji, and started chanting the Aarti in Sanskrit. Arriving in Moscow proved to be a huge surprise, as 80 people were waiting to meet me at the train station. The metaphysical "underground" arrived in full force because Igor had told them I was coming!

The Russians requested a seminar on rebirthing that very night. We did it but it was a real challenge with the translators getting across what I needed for the group breathing session the next day. We arrived the following day to a theatre building and people had come to watch! Worse still, the seats were bolted to the floor and could not be moved. I had 80 people on my hands ready to breathe and another mob that wanted to watch. I tried to explain that this was not psychodrama. I had to think fast on my feet. I told my team to take the ones who were ready and lie them down on the stage and get them going. I took the others that wanted to watch outside, and gave them a seminar postponing them until the next day.

I was on television in Russia and I was always followed by *sensitives* who were clairvoyants. I always felt like my room was bugged (which it probably was), and I was never sure if I was translated correctly on TV. It was challenging. But the miracle of it was that the rebirthers I trained in Russia rebirthed doctors after I left. The doctors wired each other up during sessions and did tests on each other. They were able to prove scientifically that rebirthing produces integrity of the brain and rejuvenation of the body. As difficult as it all was, I am proud to say the results were worth it. It is great to have science back up what we experience regularly as rebirthers!

When I took rebirthing to Russia, I had the privilege of attending an underwater birth with Charkovsky. I also conducted observations at his swimming program for newborns and had the privilege of facilitating a breathing session for Charkovsky in water. Charkovsky had a great belief in the therapeutic value of water. The baby born into water enters the world in a gentle, placid state, experiencing a *gradual* introduction into the world from liquid to liquid. Charkovsky was inspired by Tsiolkovsky, a Russian space scientist who understood where there is less gravitational pull, there is more energy available to the brain. Later Charkovsky experimented with underwater birth in the Black Sea with the presence of dolphins! Surrounded by dolphins, people cease to have fear, thus providing an excellent psychic environment for childbirth.

When we heard of the waterbirths happening in Russia (through the grapevine) in 1980, three brave rebirthers were the first to try it in the United States. Now, we actually have 130 hospitals in the U.S. that accommodate water birth! Things are changing and improving, due to pioneering midwives, parents, babies, rebirthers, and birth practitioners who continue to champion the value of laboring and birthing in water.

Markus' Path to Liberation Breathing

Someone wise said to me once, "From the moment you are born begins the long process by which you begin to die." This seemed profound until I met Sondra Ray. She said, "Thought always precedes results," therefore, "all death is suicide," based on the thought, "death is inevitable." This was a different perspective on the matter of life and death, premised on the fact that I am totally in charge of my entire destiny. I am 100 percent responsible from the moment I am conceived to the moment I pass out of this physical form…it's all up to me and my Creator together, not separately. There is no *grim reaper* beyond my control ready to strike me dead at some old age, or by some disease or accident, that on some subconscious level I have not already agreed to in advance. This was a shock to me. The power of life and death was inside of me, within the quality of my thoughts.

Through Sondra Ray I discovered some interesting facts. *How you think is how you will live. And how you live is how you will breathe.* And this breath, the most essential action of your life along with your heartbeat, coupled with consciously evolved thought, can be brought together in a remarkable healing process called rebirthing. Rebirthing can produce a powerful force to transform your life. Along with a rigorous commitment to forgiveness, you can receive the energy you need from breathwork to change any condition in your life.

In 1986, I became a rebirther in Philadelphia and began a long quest of self-introspection and inquiry. Anthony LoMastro was my first rebirther who trained me in the art. In 1987 and 1989, I travelled with Sondra Ray to India, to the sacred Divine Mother Festival of Navaratri in the Himalayas at the ashrams of Sri Sri 1008 Herakhan Babaji, the immortal "Yogi-Christ" of India written about in Yogananda's famous *Autobiography of a Yogi*. This added a deeper insight into my breathing process. Sondra had met Babaji in the flesh in His last incarnation on numerous trips to India. Now it was my time to immerse myself in the India experience.

The yogis of ancient India have known for centuries the essential relationship between Life and Breath. They developed breathing practices to make contact with the Divine, with the very Source of Life Itself. They called these practices *Pranayama* in which they would control or restrain the breath, and by doing so would raise the frequency of the mind/body to make contact with the spirit. *Prana*, or Life Force, is much more subtle than air alone…it is the very building block of life energy that permeates all things. Pranayama was designed to make direct contact with this life energy not always accessible in normal breathing. It would require years of practice and dedication. The beauty of the rebirthing breath is that it connects you with Prana without the restraint and arduous practice needed to perform the more traditional forms of Pranayama. Rebirthing is simply a deep and consciously connected, circular breath, with no holding at the top or no holding at the bottom.

When I first started the rebirthing process in 1985, I was also doing Kundalini Yoga with Yogi Bhajan, a Sikh master teacher who travelled around the country and had a following. I could see from that experience that the breath was a powerful tool of transformation. I even wore a white turban and grew my hair and beard…the reason being that Sikhs believed these were natural attributes, God given, and should not be cut. But soon, after rebirthing for a couple of years and going to India, I could see that the Sikh path of spirituality was not for me…and I did not need to look special to be spiritual. So off came the beard and the turban. It felt like liberation. Then in India the second time with Sondra Ray I received the sacred rite of Mundun, or the shaving of the head of all hair. It was a very powerful experience of surrender, to have this done on the banks of the Ganga River by the same old barber who had given Babaji His Mundun. From long hair to no hair…go figure.

I was in the vortex of a force that put all of my spiritual practices into play. Sondra had introduced many of us to *A Course in Miracles*, which she called the "most important book written in 2000 years." I began studying the lessons in the *Workbook for Students* as they became part of my rebirthing repertoire of spiritual practices. In addition, we were introduced to the Hawaiian art of forgiveness called *Ho'oponopono*, as brought to Westerners by the Hawaiian Living Treasure and Kahuna, Morrnah Simeona. She was Sondra's teacher, and we were all encouraged as rebirthers to take the class, which I did from Morrnah herself. These spiritual practices proved essential along the path I had chosen. They became the support system in which the rest of my life could unfold. They kept me sane and flowing forward. My rebirthing experience worked on very specific aspects of my relationships. For one, it got me in touch with the unresolved issues with my parents, and the past incidents from which these issues stemmed.

In 1989, I met Tara Singh, my teacher of *A Course in Miracles* for seventeen years. After meeting him all my other spiritual concerns dropped away. I knew my destiny was to be with him unequivocally. I attended his workshops and retreats for many years before we became close friends, and then we travelled together to Mexico, India, Europe, Puerto Rico, and many points around the USA. He was the one who woke me up to the power of *A Course in Miracles* and to the power of stillness and silence. Having himself spent three years in silence, he was taught directly by Dr. Helen Schucman to give the workshops on *ACIM*. Somewhere in the middle of his 25-year long mission to share the *Course*, we met at an Easter retreat he was giving in Stoney Point, New York. He penetrated my heart instantly. From 1989 to 2006 (when Tara Singh made his transition) he was my teacher, mentor, and friend. I honor his life and work in my book *Miracles with My Master, Tara Singh*. I mention this here only to fill in the space of the time I was away from rebirthing and Sondra Ray's work.

My meeting again with Sondra Ray, in 2008, seemed predestined. I was ready for a major change in my life, and a completion of a long marriage that had become a limitation for both my former wife and me. When Sondra Ray arrived back in my life in January of 2008, I had no idea what was in store for me. It felt like forces greater than myself were putting us together for a Divine purpose. All I needed to do was not to resist the forward movement, and not hang on to anything from the past. My teacher Tara Singh had once asked his teacher, Krishnamurti, "Does Life take care?" to which he replied, "Yes, when you completely let go." My only question was, "Can I completely let go?"

Within three months my old life was done, and Sondra and I were on a plane to Greece to teach an LRT®, then India to lead a group of thirty-five students on the Divine Mother's India Quest. I was going back to Babaji's ashram, Haidakhan, where I had shaved my head in a ceremony on the banks of the Ganga River almost twenty years earlier (in 1989, the same year I met my teacher of *A Course in Miracles*, Tara Singh). I seemed to be making a complete circle in my spiritual journey. When we arrived in Haidakhan, Muniraj, the guru in residence, greeted us coming up the road from his jeep. His smile was from ear to ear, and I felt intense joy to be *coming home*.

It was no accident to be embracing rebirthing again, to be the consort of Sondra Ray, and to be smack dab back in Haidakhan in a matter of a few months. My return to this form of spiritual purification using the breath was in keeping with Tara Singh's emphasis on pranayama with me, though a much different and simpler form. I was back in the sphere of influence of India, Sondra Ray, and Babaji.

Today, Sondra and I lead an annual pilgrimage called India Quest to the Spring Divine Mother Festival (Navaratri) at Haidakhan. Liberation Breathing® continues to be Sondra's defining teaching tool, as well as immersion in the Indian culture. The countrywide Divine Mother Festival introduces Westerners to paying homage to the most basic Force of Nature, the Divine Mother. Though in a Hindu context, the Navaratri is universal in its intent to honor Life itself.

How Liberation Breathing Evolved

Liberation Breathing® from the Divine Mother was entrusted to Sondra Ray because of her unrivaled dedication to the rebirthing movement, coupled with her love for Babaji, India, and the Divine Mother. I was entrusted with it as well. It became more and more clear to us that the Divine Mother was the Force behind our work, including the breathwork we called rebirthing. We came to honor that by reading the Divine Mother names in each session, repeating a Divine Mother mantra, and invoking the Divine Mother energy as a means of support for those breathing. We meditated for over a year on the name Liberation Breathing® and began to introduce the Divine Mother into breathing sessions in this way. We were told that by doing this the sessions became nine times more powerful. We flew to India to confirm with our gurus this evolutionary shift, and afterwards we registered the name with the U.S. Patent Office. In the fall of 2009, Liberation Breathing® from the Divine Mother was officially born.

The Father of Rebirthing, Babaji, (as channeled through Leonard Orr) had now passed the new expression of this work through the Divine Mother—Liberation Breathing (as channeled through Sondra Ray). Our relationship was at the foundation of this shift. It represented a surrender of sorts for me to accept the Divine Mother as my guide and support. Sondra was my wife, but the Divine Mother was the Force that brought us together to work and live in a new frequency for relationships. We were to master the state of no-conflict so important to worship of the Divine Mother.

Together our mission became one of Divine service. Teaching Liberation Breathing® still incorporates the foundations of rebirthing and relationship dynamics as taught in the LRT®. It also incorporates a deep spiritual aspect hitherto unseen. Liberation Breathing® now has the means to cope with aspects of problems and experiences beyond the practices of good "processing" and "case cracking." The breath, one of the angels of the Divine Mother, invokes Her help directly, beyond our thinking, to impart the mercy of healing sought by all. In the space beyond thought, in the fifth dimension of miracles, Liberation Breathing® now placed its ultimate practice and trust in the hands of the Divine.

In addition to reading the Divine Mother names in the sessions, Sondra and I took them into our daily spiritual practice. We read them out loud every day before starting any task, along with the lesson of the day from *A Course in Miracles*, and our Ho'oponopono cleansing. Here in Bali, where I am writing this, we are inspired by the culture that honors the Divine Mother every day with a small offering before starting their day. We keep an altar in our home and put flowers next to pictures and statues that honor the Divine Mother. Even when we travel we take these pictures with us, and set up an altar in our room and in the place where we teach. Liberation Breathing® is a sacrament, and as harbingers of this sacrament we are entrusted with honoring its Source, the Divine Mother. Because we read the names every day, it feels only natural to read them in the sessions. We always ask the client permission first, and they always say, "Yes!"

Part 4

The Guiding Lights of Liberation Breathing

A Speech by Babaji

Love and serve all humanity.
Assist everyone.
Be cheerful. Be courteous.
Be a dynamo of irrepressible happiness.
See God and good in every face.
There is no Saint without a past,
There is no sinner without a future.
Praise every soul.
If you cannot praise someone,
Let them pass out of your life.
Be original. Be inventive.
Dare, dare, and dare more.
Do not imitate. Stand on your own ground.
Do not lean on the borrowed staff of others.
Think your own thoughts.
Be yourself.
All perfection and all virtues of
God are hidden inside you.
Reveal them.
The Savior, also, is already within you.
Reveal Him.
Let His grace emancipate you.
Let your life be that of a rose;
Though silent, it speaks in the language of fragrance.

Babaji

> If you see him who has not been born of a woman, throw your
> face on the ground and worship him, for he is your Father.
> —*The Gospel of St. Thomas*

In many sacred texts it is written that when righteousness declines, God creates for Himself a body and comes to live on Earth. He appears and makes Himself known to those who seek him. Babaji is one such emanation of the Divine, who, out of compassion, appears in human form—repeatedly over the centuries—to urge humanity to progress on the path of "Truth, simplicity, love, and service to mankind."

In fulfillment of ancient scriptural and prophetic predictions, Babaji manifested a youthful body in 1970 in a cave near the village of Haidakhan in the Kumaon foothills of the Himalayas. He then climbed to the top of Mount Kailash where He sat for 45 days without sleeping, eating, or drinking. After this intense period of meditation, He began to teach His message to villagers who gathered around him.

His home in Northern India, also known as Herakhan, is considered the birthplace of yogis, the source of Divine inspiration, and the ancestral home of Lord Shiva. Babaji spoke of Haidakhan as "the holiest place in the world, holier even than Benares. The water of this river [Ganga] purifies you from all sins. By merely sitting here you reap the results of hundreds of lifetimes of penance. Those who live here for some time automatically gain yogic powers. Those who have darshan at this place will have all their wishes fulfilled. They will have the assurance of complete success. But only he can come here in whose life a turning point has come, when the spiritual energy is rising." During the 1970s and 1980s he oversaw the construction and expansion of the Haidakhan ashram and gardens, where thousands of guests now visit each year, especially during the Spring Divine Mother Festival known as Navaratri.

Babaji was accessible for 14 years in his last physical form. And yet, He has not left, because in reality He does not "come and go." He was and is omnipresent. His form is limitless and beyond the scope of time. He teaches though vibration and direct experience. Babaji is beyond religion. He teaches that all faiths ultimately lead to the same goal. He is the essence of all religions. He transcends every belief.

He teaches that through the practice of Karma Yoga (work dedicated to God) man purifies and protects oneself. He teaches a philosophy of action. "Work is worship," and "An idle man is a dead man," are two quotes he often spoke. To experience Him answers all questions. He is available for you as he is for all.

Radhe Shyam, a U.S. State Department administrator, lived for five years with Babaji in Haidakhan. In his book *I am Harmony* Shyam writes:

"Babaji is a spiritual being who serves constantly as a link between the Formless Divine and the physical creation, between God and humankind. He states that He is a manifestation of Lord Shiva, one of the names India gives to The Divine—a form of God known as a renunciate, a helper, and the greatest of Teachers…People see Him in many roles—as Lord Shiva, the Supreme Guru, purifier, friend, the Divine Child, the Divine Mother, Divine Father, Supreme Yogi, a healer, an Immortal. He is all of these things and we see in Him that for which we look. We also see ourselves in Him, for He mirrors each of us, so we can see where we are on our Paths and gain insight into ourselves and what we need to work on…His chief concern is with the human spirit or soul—that in humankind which is closest to the Divine, which carries the spark of The Divine. He teaches that the Creator and all of the Creation is One." (ix-x)

Paramahansa Yogananda calls Babaji the "Yogi-Christ of Modern India" in his 1946 book *Autobiography of a Yogi* (available at www.ananda.org). Yogananda writes:

"That there is no historical reference to Babaji need not surprise us. The great guru has never openly appeared in any century; the misinterpreting glare of publicity has no place in his millennial plans. Like the Creator, the sole but silent Power, Babaji works in a humble obscurity.

"Great prophets like Christ and Krishna come to earth for a specific and spectacular purpose; they depart as soon as it is accomplished. Other avatars, like Babaji, undertake work which is concerned more with the slow evolutionary progress of man during the centuries than with any one outstanding event of history. Such masters always veil themselves from the gross public gaze, and have the power to become invisible at will. For these reasons, and because they generally instruct their disciples to maintain silence about them, a number of towering spiritual figures remain world-unknown. I give in these pages on Babaji merely a hint of his life." (Chapter 33)

There is a ceremonial prayer called the Aarti, "The Offering of Light," which is sung in Sanskrit. One of the lines I love the most from it is this: "Thou are a never failing spring of bliss." That is and always has been my experience of Babaji, who has been with us on earth in human form countless times since life began. Some of His lifetimes are well known—Shiva, Ram, and Krishna, for example. In other lifetimes He was known to relatively few. Jesus is said to have visited Babaji in Benares during Jesus' travel and studies in the East. It was there that Babaji shaved Jesus' head and blessed Him before Jesus started His ministry. Babaji Himself told me this.

The Mantra "Om Namah Shivay"

Babaji taught that the simplest and most powerful method for bringing peace and understanding to the mind is through singing or saying of the Lord's name. He said: "This is the Mahamantra—Om Namah Shivay— the great original mantra given by the Lord to humanity. Everyone should repeat it. It can be given to everyone, and everything can be achieved through it. The power of this mantra is infinite. This mantra is more powerful than the atom bomb."

Om Namah Shivay means:
- I take refuge in God.
- I surrender to Shiva, that part of God that destroys my ignorance.
- Infinite Being, Infinite Manifestation, Infinite Spirit.

Babaji said, "The Lord's name is like Divine nectar—Amrita. Repeat it all the time. Om Namah Shivay."

My Road To Babaji

In a recent meditation, I saw myself coming toward Babaji for several lifetimes. It was a very winding, curvy, difficult road and at the end of the experience I saw myself on a straight road going directly to him. Who knows how long this has taken? It was exhilarating.

A false master is a tranquilizer. You come to him and he consoles you. A true spiritual master such as Babaji helps you grow rapidly. With growth, you have to pass through many difficulties. A true master will haunt you. There is no transformation without fire. Friction is the right word for the inner war. You become uprooted so your past no longer has power over your mind. All that has been before must be disrupted.

Unless you are ready to encounter yourself, you cannot become a disciple. A master can do nothing if you are not ready to face yourself. All that you have denied and repressed will come up and that gives one fear. You only become a disciple when you are ready to expose your whole being to yourself. I always felt totally exposed around Babaji, but he was the most exciting thing on Earth.

The Master is also a midwife, helping you pass through a new birth and be reborn. You have to trust. You cannot doubt. You have to drop your armor completely. The openness has to be total. Otherwise nothing happens. To me, it is the greatest training on Earth. At times I have felt like I am in training for the Olympics.

The Master is the one who awakens you. He wants to birth you into His or Her dimension. When there is a Master like Jesus or Babaji, people try to escape from him in every way possible. People rationalize their escape and find clever reasons why they are escaping. They find something wrong with the master. They avoid the master because they are not willing to go through fear (which is why we use breathwork). When you encounter him he can see right through you and the false life you made up. You become transparent to him or her. You cannot hide yourself. You cannot hide the falseness that you are. I used to become a trembling leaf before Babaji. I had to become courageous to be around him. When I took the jump into the abyss, I gained everything.

Babaji always said: "My love is available to you. You can take it or not." If you postpone the entry, your mind remains the same. People try to change themselves in every way. *Is there really much change?* The Master is freedom. The Master is fire. You become completely liquid so that all that is wrong is burned. Babaji is the furnace. At times I would feel like my bones were on fire for weeks on end. I knew this fire purification was what I needed. The past must die for the true future to be born. We have remained in prison so long that we think that is our home. The Master has escaped. He will help you escape, but you have to be vulnerable. I came out different from what I was. A transformation is a discontinuity from the past, it is not patchwork. If you are courageous enough to pass through the fire, a new world will open before you.

Note: Some people have a problem with the idea of a "guru" as they think it is a "go between" them and God. This is not the case with Babaji. He descended directly from the Source, so He could never be a go between, which is why I chose Him as my guide.

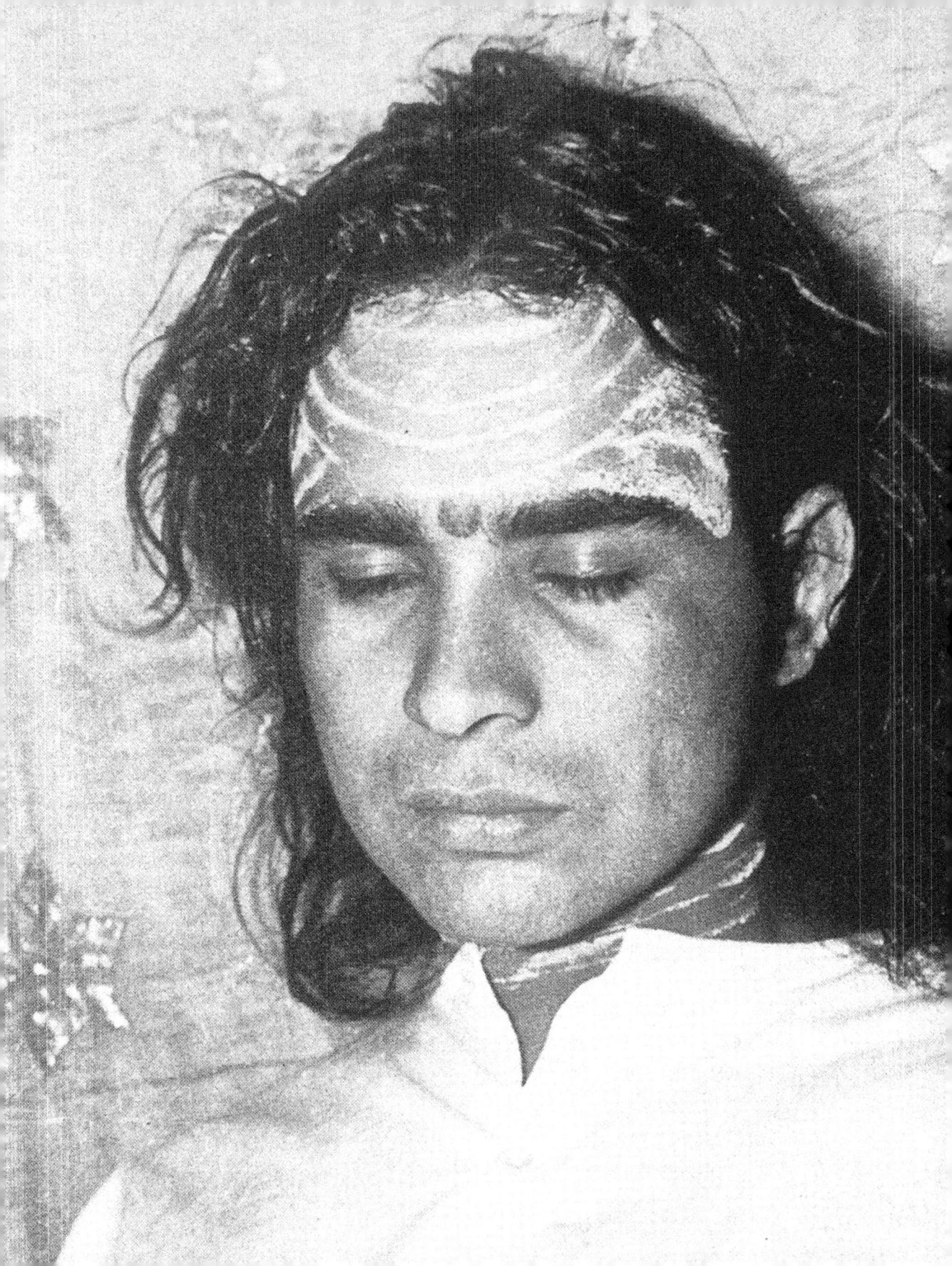

The Divine Mother

At my request, A Yogi friend, Harigovind of Switzerland, wrote the following:

"To write about the Divine Mother resembles the attempt to empty the ocean with a teacup, for she is omnipotent, omnipresent, omniscient. The Mother is supreme—supreme power, supreme wisdom, supreme peace. The original spark of creation is a feminine aspect. Name her electricity, name her gravity, name her space.

"We must not only recognize God in the Father form or only in the Mother form as Mary. We must come to recognize the Divine Mother in all her forms. She teaches us to be in our compassionate side—the side that honors all life. The Divine Mother is the one substance—the substratum of every communication, of every creation, of every display of power and beauty. She is the origin of consciousness, all the elements, all the laws of physics, mathematics, music, economics, and language. She is the primordial cause of all existence and eternally one with Shiva, the simple Father (Babaji).

"In the West, the absence of the Divine Mother in image and experience has resulted in our orientation becoming lopsided and out of balance. We can see proof of that in the massive threat of nuclear war, pollution, and destruction of our forests. The real solution to all of these problems can lie only in a shift of consciousness, in a reorientation of the mind. A new orientation to the Divine Mother's energy, a turning to higher wisdom is needed."

The great saint Sri Aurobindo said that "surrender to the Divine Mother is the final stage of perfection." It took me a long time to figure out that the "secret" of the saints and masters that I had met, who could perform so many miracles, was just that: surrender to a worship of the Divine Mother. That is why in India it is said that there is nothing higher than worship of the Divine Mother. From this they gained real power and supernatural abilities. She is just as available to all.

It is said that the Divine Mother releases us from delusion. This is of maximum importance on the spiritual path. To make rapid spiritual progress, one must reach for the deep, called MA (the internal) rather than MAYA (the external). The sooner we do that, the better for ourselves, and the whole planet. The more you surrender to the Divine Mother, the faster you progress.

She will bring us to the nurturing, tender aspects of ourselves, which are so needed to solve the problems of the world today. The Divine Mother will give us the solutions both to our personal problems and to our planetary problems. We need to let her teach us how. We want to avert catastrophe in our relationships, our bodies, our societies, and our countries. How do we deal with the shadows in ourselves and in our societies? Logic cannot always find the answer, but the feminine side of our selves is more capable of harmonizing the light and the shadow. Extraordinary changes take place when the goddess is accepted for women and men alike! I have interviewed many men whose lives were completely changed by surrendering to the Divine Mother.

Since the Goddess has not been an integral part of Western life for the last two thousand years, we as her children are rather maladjusted. The Goddess, or Divine Mother, leads us in the way of natural law, wisdom, and unconditional love; however, we do not pay enough attention to this aspect of God. That may be because of old beliefs that the Goddess is pagan and heathen. This is most unfortunate, because we then overlook her beneficial, life-enhancing, and regenerative powers and her offer for renewal. In Liberation Breathing® she offers us renewal!

Although pure formless deity has no gender, the expressions of God as Divine masculine and Divine feminine are like the right and left hands of God. To emphasize the masculine more, as we have done with the patriarchy, puts us out of balance. Too often we use our bodies to rebel against the "negative mother," whereas if we could surrender to the Divine Mother, our bodies could be used as instruments to channel the natural infinite love and intelligence needed, not only to experience bliss, but to access the purest wisdom.

The Divine Mother is a spiritual channel we should enjoy. *Who wouldn't want sexuality radiating through the whole body as a healing force igniting one's being with light? How do we begin to experience the Divine Mother right now?* Everything we possess is a gift of the Divine Mother. Begin by expressing more appreciation to the source of life and paying homage to the highest of the high.

> *Praise to you Great Mother.*
> *Make our lives a miracle.*
> *Show us what to do and how to do it.*
> *Let us be innocent and receptive, like a child.*
> *Make our hearts Your temple.*
> *I pray that the people will surrender to you in*
> *Liberation Breathing, as You called it.*

Presently there is a reawakening of the sacred feminine in the hearts and minds of people throughout the world, and that is partly due to the presence of Ammachi on the earth. That is why we are so fortunate to have her here on the earth at this time. She is surely an aspect of the Divine Mother in form, and she is available in the body for you to meet. When Babaji took conscious departure he stated, "I am leaving everything in the hands of the Divine Mother." Then, he started sending us all to Ammachi.

Ammachi

Holy Mother Amritanandamayi lives today as India's leading female light—an esteemed and stupendous incarnation of the Divine Mother herself. She selflessly travels the world to console, hug, heal, and inspire millions with the power of Divine Love. I am one of her fortunate children, and I have no words to express the inner joy I feel when just thinking of her. Every day she takes into her lap thousands and thousands of people of all ages, religions, races, and walks of life. She absorbs all suffering and negativity into her body. She blesses us all and heals us with her gentle caresses. "The lady of love, simply known as 'Amma' may be the greatest phenomenon in the history of religion," it has been said. I agree that she certainly has emerged as one of the most powerful spiritual masters ever to walk the planet. Although she was a child prodigy, she had to go through a difficult childhood. She walked and spoke at age six months, and sang to Lord Krishna right away.

Her presence is always a potent blessing-force opening us up and infusing our spiritual energy centers. Her body vibrates with the tremendous power (shakti) of Divine love. It is like she is connected to an electrical current that supercharges her biological structure. She is a living fountain of grace, and we all feel incredulous at our good fortune to be near her Divinity in human form. Many consider her to be like a female Christ who helps release us from old wounds and karmic bonds and awakens us to Divine Spirit.

Below is an important message by Amma from her speech titled "The Awakening of Universal Motherhood," given in Geneva on October 7, 2002:

"…What today's world really needs is cooperation between men and women, based on a firm sense of unity in the family and society. Wars and conflict, all the suffering and lack of peace in the present-day world, will certainly lessen to a great extent if women and men begin to cooperate and to support each other. Unless harmony is restored between the masculine and the feminine, between men and women, peace will continue to be no more than a distant dream…

"The language of the heart, the language of love, which is related to the feminine principle, is quite different. Those who speak this language do not care about their ego. They have no interest in proving that they are right or that anyone else is wrong. They are deeply concerned about their fellow beings and wish to help, support, and uplift others. In their presence transformation simply happens. They are the givers of tangible hope and of light in this world. Those who approach them are reborn. When such people speak it is not to lecture, to impress, or to argue—it is a true communion of hearts.

"Real love has nothing to do with lust or self-centeredness. In real love, you are not important; the other is important. In love, the other is not your instrument to fulfill your selfish desires; you are an instrument of the Divine with the intention of doing good in the world. Love does not sacrifice others; love gives joyfully of itself. Love is selfless—but not the enforced selflessness of women being pushed in the background, treated as objects. In real love, you do not feel worthless; on the contrary, you expand and become one with everything—all-encompassing, ever blissful…

"The essence of motherhood is not restricted to women who have given birth; it is a principle inherent in both women and men. It is an attitude of the mind. It is love—and that love is the very breath of life…for those in whom motherhood has awakened, love and compassion for everyone is as much part of their being as breathing. The forthcoming age should be dedicated to reawakening the healing power of motherhood. This is the only way to realize our dream of peace and harmony for all. And it can be done! It is entirely up to us. Let us remember this and move forward."

The Words of Amma

"Each one of you has the beauty and power of a saint or a sage. Each one of you is an infinite source of power. Yet when you see a saint or sage, you recoil, saying, "No this is for special people. I can't do it. I have my own little tiny world to bother about and that's enough for me. Divinity is none of my business." This kind of attitude will never help you to come out of the small, hard shell of your little ego. This is why the Vedanta tells us to contemplate the Veda dictum: "I am Brahman (Absolute Reality). I am God. I am the Universe. I am absolute power, the totality of consciousness, which makes everything beautiful and full of light and life.""

"God is the hidden formula of life. But you won't feel Him unless you call Him. His glory and splendor are ever present, but unrevealed because you have not invoked the power of His Presence through prayer and meditation."

"The moment of revelation that has occurred to many great souls can happen to you as well. Everybody is being prepared to reach this final state of dropping all ego. It must happen because that is the final stage of evolution. You cannot avoid it. The final destiny for all souls is the dropping away of every obstruction to peace and contentment. When that moment comes, the ego is dropped, and you won't struggle anymore; you will just bow down and surrender."

"You can raise a hundred objections to the theory of karma. Still the law of karma is operating in your life. It has you in its grip. Children, our actions will return to each one of us, whether one is a believer or non-believer. Karma is like a boomerang. Newborn babies are sometimes physically deformed or mentally retarded. Are such events accidental? No!"

"Each thing that happens in life has a cause. Sometimes the cause is visible and at other times it is not. Sometimes the cause is to be found in the immediate past; but in some cases it stems from the remote past. Nothing is accidental. Nature is not accidental. Creation is not an accident. Our past is not just the past of this lifetime. The past is also all previous lifetimes through which we have traveled in different names and forms. We must be alert and careful about what we do today because we do not know what effect it will produce tomorrow. Your negative feelings will invoke the negative feelings of others. They too will suffer, thereby adding to the storehouse of their karma."

"Contentment ensues from egolessness. And egolessness comes from devotion, love, and utter surrender to the Supreme Lord. An ordinary devotee wants to keep his ego, whereas a true devotee wants to die to his ego so that he can live in consciousness of pure innocent love. Dying to the ego…makes you immortal. Death of the ego leads you to deathlessness. When the ego dies, you live eternally in bliss."

Jesus and A Course in Miracles

A Course in Miracles is the most important book written in 2000 years.
—Sondra Ray

What would you do if you knew there was someone who knew all the answers to all problems… someone who had mastered life completely…someone who could put you into instant joy…someone who could heal you…someone who had even conquered death? Would you go find him? What would you do if you knew Jesus was still around and you could find Him? Would you check Him out, even if you were not raised a Christian? I would think you might.

What would you do if you knew there was a book written by Him in the last few decades? A book for modern times…a book that cleared up all the confusion about religion…a book that explained everything, answered all questions, and taught you how to heal yourself completely…a book that taught you how to have perfect relationships? What if the book itself was a miracle? Would you read it?

That book is here. Jesus is here through it. The answers are in it. That book is *A Course in Miracles*, and it is available now. You can be healed now. Imagine having Liberation Breathing®, *A Course in Miracles* (Jesus), Babaji, and Ammachi all in your life! That is what I have, and that is what you can have. You can receive salvation now. Your life can work now.

Personally, I think it is important to learn from someone who has mastered what we are trying to learn. The problem with learning from someone like Jesus is that one has to confront all their feelings on the subject of God and religion…not an easy topic because of all the confusion, memories of religious wars, and so forth. That is why Jesus dictated this book (through Dr. Helen Schucman, a clinical psychologist working at Columbia University in the late 1960s) to correct the mistakes of religion.

Do you know that the foundation of Christianity was actually written down 30 years after Jesus' death, and that much of it was written in a way that can be easily misinterpreted, since it was written through their egos? The ego is based on the thought that one is separate from God. It would be possible for anyone who had that thought to write something deceptive. In other words, we cannot be separate from God. If there is a belief that you are separate at the center of a thought system, the whole thing can be deceptive.

Maybe it is time to re-examine all your religious conditioning, keeping that which is appropriate and forgiving that which was mixed up and riddled with guilt. *A Course in Miracles* is not a religion. It is a correction of religion.

Ken Wapnick is one of the world's leading experts on *A Course in Miracles*, and a respected teacher for me. He shares that the presence of Jesus on the planet was so pure and it purged so much ego, that it has taken 2,000 years to process it. Now, after that time, we are ready to hear the next words from Him. Now Jesus is saying, "You did not understand me before. I am going to give you another chance. I will explain what I was saying then in another way."

Using A Course in Miracles

A Course in Miracles is designed perfectly and should be read according to the directions in the "Preface," "Introduction," and *Manual for Teachers*. Reading ahead to parts for which one has not had proper preparation may stir up the ego and cause discomfort. To make it easy on yourself, you might find it helpful to join a local study group.

Originally *A Course in Miracles* was published in three parts: the *Text*, the *Workbook for Students*, and the *Manual for Teachers*. The *Text* provides the theoretical basis for Jesus' teachings; the *Workbook for Students* provides practical lessons to be undertaken by the student, one per day for one year. These lessons have very specific instructions designed to give the student grounded experiences in everyday life which apply the principles the *Text* presents. The *Manual for Teachers* provides a glossary of terms and commonly asked questions that may arise while undertaking the lessons.

Although the *Text* is essential to the understanding of what Jesus is saying, it is the practice of the lessons in the *Workbook for Students* which will give the student the most immediate and lasting transformation.

To give you an idea of what the *Text* is like, I have randomly chosen one paragraph below. Every paragraph is equally as powerful. Notice how much food for thought is here. Take time to digest it.

"No right mind can believe that its will is stronger than God's. If then, a mind believes that its will is different from His, it can only decide either that there is no God or that God's Will is fearful. The former accounts for the atheist, and the latter for the martyr who believes that God demands sacrifices. Either of these insane decisions will induce panic, because the atheist believes that he is alone, and the martyr that God is crucifying him." (T9 I. 8:1-4)

How many people feel abandoned by God and therefore project there is no God? Or, that God is not approving of them, and therefore they must sacrifice in order to get God's approval? The paragraph above makes clear that these two positions cannot be the will of God, which is perfect happiness for you. Now let us take an example from the *Workbook for Students*:

Lesson 190: I choose the joy of God instead of pain.

The *Workbook for Students* explanation of this lesson is beautiful: "Pain is a sign that in his mind illusions reign [the ego's belief that pain is natural] in place of truth." Pain means one is mistaken in his thinking. The fact is that God's will for you is total joy and absolutely no pain. A person in pain is indulging in the ego. The main point is that nothing external can hurt you. Only your mind, and often your subconscious mind, can cause you pain. No one but yourself affects you. There is nothing in the world that has the power to dominate you, make you ill, or cause you sadness. But you are also the one who has the power to change your mind. The world you see does nothing. It merely represents your thoughts and it will change as you change your mind…and choose the joy of God as what you want.

The *Workbook* further explains: "It is your thoughts alone that cause you pain. Nothing external to your mind can hurt or injure you in any way." When one is in pain, one is denying God. But if you do lay down your thoughts of danger, fear, attack, and judgment of yourself, you will begin to find a world without pain. Pain is illusion. Joy is reality. Pain is deception; joy alone is truth. The lesson concludes: "And so again we make the only choice that can ever be made; we choose between illusions and truth, or pain and joy, or hell and heaven."

Another lesson I like is Lesson 101: "God's will for me is perfect happiness." That may be the opposite of what you were taught in church. Usually we got the impression that God's will for us was to suffer, and that is how we could be holy. We were taught we were "sinners" who would have to repent to prevent some catastrophe of punishment in our afterlife. We would go to heaven or hell based on this repentance. However, real repentance is seeing that you are eternally innocent in the first place, and that nothing you ever did affected this innocence in God's eyes. There is no sin in your reality; it exists only in your "ego's world" that was made up in separation from God. This world is not a true representation of Divine reality.

Lesson 101: *"God's Will for you is perfect happiness because there is no sin, and suffering is causeless. Joy is just, and pain is but the sign you have misunderstood yourself. Fear not the Will of God. But turn to it in confidence that it will set you free from all the consequences sin has wrought in feverish imagination. Say: God's Will for me is perfect happiness. There is no sin; it has no consequence."*

Pain and suffering is often what the ego uses to "pay" for some deep feeling of guilt about something that happened in the past. The belief in "sin" is a request for some form of suffering or punishment, and even death. This all happens very swiftly on the subconscious level. So if God's will for me is perfect happiness, and forgiveness is always justified, then there is no room for sin, guilt and death in my *real mind*. I made up this awful scenario of sin-guilt-punishment-pain-and-death. Therefore, in God's eyes, there is no consequence of punishment now, or in the "afterlife," because His will for you and me is *only* happiness. Why not start thinking this way: "Since only happiness is God's will for me, I will forgive everything in my life that does not bring me pure joy!" This is the real stairway to heaven. Through forgiveness you can ascend to heaven right now.

Overcoming Resistance to A Course in Miracles

There may be a tremendous resistance to *A Course in Miracles* at first. This is your ego rearing its ugly head. Go beyond it. As your ego dissolves, you will begin to see how the books make a lot of sense. Later, I even said, "This is the only thing that makes sense to me!" The early lessons of *A Course in Miracles* are confronting to your ego, but for a good reason. Your ego must fall apart before it can be replaced with the Christ mind, which is your real mind. Eventually you may even crave reading the lessons in a wonderful way.

If you are resisting *A Course in Miracles*, ask yourself:
- Am I afraid of having it all and feeling good?
- Am I choosing pain over joy?
- Am I too addicted to my negativity to recognize a good thing like this?
- Am I angry with God and fed up with anything in a religious tone?
- Am I attached to my religious conditioning, even though it does not bring me real inner joy?
- Am I stubborn, rebellious, or loving my misery?

If you answer yes to any of these, you may have convinced yourself you do not need *A Course in Miracles*, and/or you should not read it. Or you gave up on reading it. All I am asking is, "Are you willing to see this differently?"

If you have not purchased *A Course in Miracles*, I hope you will. If you have had the books and have not opened them, I hope you will. If you have started and you quit on a certain lesson, I hope you will go back to that lesson and start again. One of the things that helped me remember to do the lesson each day was to write the lesson in the palm of my hand in ballpoint. Then I would notice it from time to time. If you choose to try Liberation Breathing,® sooner or later your practitioner will recommend a section from *A Course in Miracles* based on what would be extremely helpful to your situation.

Markus' Study of A Course in Miracles with Tara Singh

I met Tara Singh during a retreat over the Easter weekend of 1989. Clearly, he was to be my teacher of this remarkable scripture. I attended his workshops and retreats for many years before we became close friends, and then we travelled together to Mexico, India, Europe, Puerto Rico, and many points around the U.S. He was the one who woke me up to the power of *A Course in Miracles* and to the power of stillness and silence.

Tara Singh had been J. Krishnamurti's student for over 25 years and had himself spent three years in silence when he met Dr. Helen Schucman, the scribe of *A Course in Miracles*, in New York City, a few years after it was published. She trained him to give lectures and workshops on *A Course in Miracles*, and put him through two and a half years of mentoring in which she totally dismantled his ego, and introduced him to his true function in life. He called her every day at the same time, from wherever he was in the world. It was she who said to him, "*A Course in Miracles* is to be lived, not to be learned." By this she meant any truth, such as held within Jesus's teaching in this book, has to be applied in your life in order for it to have any meaning. Mere intellectualism cannot transform a person, which is what *A Course in Miracles* is meant to do. Learning of a truth, such as "God's peace and joy are mine," (Lesson 105), is not our truth unless it is lived, and we actually are in that state of peace and joy all of the time.

The means for bringing *A Course in Miracles* into application are clearly laid out in the *Course* itself. It gives the principles of miracles, self-transformation, forgiveness, overcoming the common emotions of fear and anger, and replacing special relationships with holy relationships all within the main Text. It gives 365 lessons in the Workbook for Students to make these principles a practical function of your life. It takes one year, one lesson per day, to complete the Workbook for Students, at which point most people continue to review the lessons again and again. *A Course in Miracles* is a spiritual spring that never runs dry. Once you start it you feel it is "for the rest of your life." It provides the means for us to replace the ego-based self we made up with the spirit-based Self that God created us to be. In short, *A Course in Miracles* introduces us to our Divine

Self Identity. When we fully realize and live by this Self, we are liberated from all pain, sorrow, problems and even death.

Tara Singh had the ability to bring his mind, and the minds of those to whom he spoke, to silence and stillness. He demonstrated what any lesson of *A Course in Miracles* is meant to do. When the lesson says, "The stillness of the peace of God is mine," (Lesson 273), he would bring himself and others to that inner state of stillness and peace. He demonstrated it in no uncertain terms. Anyone in his field of influence would insist on bringing the lessons of *A Course in Miracles* into application. Of course I had a lot of shadows to undo, ones that were preventing me from living by the principles of the *Course*. Most of these shadows escaped my awareness. This is why it is helpful to have a living teacher who can help you undo these deep-seeded patterns, such as conditioning from family, religion, education and society that prevent true liberation from the ego self. Otherwise full application is not so easy, or even possible.

My training with Tara Singh gave me a deep appreciation of *A Course in Miracles* and the process one must undertake for inner transformation. Tara Singh would call this process, "a love for inner correction." It is not for the faint of heart, or for those not willing to take the introspective journey of self-examination. But for anyone who is on fire to know the higher truth of LIFE....and, to know his or her divine Self, *A Course in Miracles* is a roadmap to this region of Self Realization.

Liberation Breathing®, in conjunction with a serious study of *A Course in Miracles*, helps a person replace the self the ego made with the Self God created. Over and over again we see the transformative power of this conjunction. In 1985, I was introduced to the *Course* by Sondra Ray. She said, "*A Course in Miracles* is the most important book written in 2000 years." That got my attention. Then I went on to study for 17 years with the man Dr. Schucman had groomed to work with serious students, Tara Singh. I yearned to be that real student, like he had been to his teachers. Tara Singh took me to places in mind, body, and spirit I would never have known without his grace. He was my master; he was my teacher. As Jesus would say, we are both teacher and student to one another. This Holy Relationship is the subject of a book I have almost completed:

Miracles With My Master: Tara Singh. As he would say, *A Course in Miracles* is "A Gift for All Mankind," and the greatest contribution America has made to the world, barring no other contribution.

Sondra and I now work with *A Course in Miracles* with our students, encourage many around the world to make it part of their daily spiritual practice, and help others glean the teaching of the Christ in ways that conventional religion could never do. *A Course in Miracles* is a "correction" of false thinking from which we were conditioned. It liberates us, along with Liberation Breathing®, from all negativity in the mind that is blocking our awareness of who we are. Love is who we really are, and that absolute state of Being is now accessible to us through Liberation Breathing® and a serious study of *A Course in Miracles*. The *Course* and Liberation Breathing® give miracles that reverse our thinking and remove the blocks we have imposed to avoid knowing our true Self.

For students who wish to hear some of our commentaries on *A Course in Miracles*, you can subscribe to our website MiraclesArePresent.com and receive new posts, as well as listen to dialogues and lectures from the past few years. We invite you into this world of Liberation Breathing®, *A Course in Miracles*, and the principles of *A Course in Miracles*. It is a dynamic combination that will undoubtedly transform your life for the better.

When Dr. Schucman was in the last days of her life, she spoke these words to Tara Singh: "I give you the *Course*, and it is for the rest of your life." He went on for over 25 years to write books, teach serious students, give workshops and lectures on *A Course in Miracles* and other great beings and their words and lives of wisdom. His emphasis was always on application, the living of wisdom, rather than the mere intellectual learning of it. He took his students to a spaciousness inside themselves "beyond the words," where the stillness and the peace of God could actually be felt and experienced. You can explore more of Tara Singh's work, writings, and teachings at www.JosephPlan.org. For students who want to begin immediate study of *A Course in Miracles*, the entire book in English is available free of charge at: acim-search.miraclevision.com/std-second-edition-and-supps/index.html

Morrnah Simeona: The Hawaiian Wisdom of Ho'oponopono

Ho'oponopono is an ancient Hawaiian Kahuna prayer and one of the greatest gifts Hawaiian culture has given to mankind. The name itself means "setting right." My Kahuna teacher, Morrnah Nalamaku Simeona, was the one who made it available in a modernized version for our time. The Ho'oponopono process provides a step-by-step approach to achieving peace, balance, and a new means of life through the understanding of one's self identity. Ho'oponopono is a process for:

- maintaining good relationships not only among family, friends, and colleagues, but also with the supernatural powers
- problem-solving
- releasing the negative effects of past and present actions in our lives by spiritually, mentally, and physically cleansing through the processes of repentance, forgiveness, and transmutation
- righting errors and creating balance
- making right any stressful relationship or situation in life and freeing tensions created in these relationships
- looking at ourselves to see how we contributed to the problem
- conflict resolution
- embracing spiritual truths, thus lending dignity to the process of conflict resolution

LB® practitioners are required to become familiar with Ho'oponopono. This is so the practitioner can better maintain his or her own clarity. Practitioners also encourage clients to learn it, as it is amazing and in total harmony with the breathing. By practicing Ho'oponopono, the LB® practitioner is not only clearer, he or she can also clear things for the client by doing the prayer in advance of the session. This is very supportive to the client and it works because the practitioner acknowledges that any toxic and destructive thought forms in the client's mind are also in his or her mind. By taking 100 percent responsibility for these thoughts, and neutralizing them through Ho'oponopono, both the practitioner and the client are freed from undesirable consequences they may cause, simultaneously.

Ho'oponopono Experience in Hawaii

We head for Pu'uhonua o Honaunau, the City of Refuge, where historically those condemned and sentenced to punishment went to be absolved of their errors and receive Atonement. The sacredness of Hawaii comes over us in full force. The road winds through lava fields sloping down to the sea. At the edge of the water we stop to hear our Hawaiian guide's stories of this place, its history and function in the ancient culture. The sandy beach is soft under our feet, and we can imagine the Hawaiian ali'i, or chieftan royalty, populating the area and walking the grounds as keepers of the Mana, or Holy Life Force that kept all of nature and society in harmony.

What impresses us most is the fact that people who committed serious crimes could come here to be forgiven. Our guide points out that the ali'i chiefs guarded the entrance to the sacred structures, preventing easy entry by land. In order to reach the Pu'uhonua, or the Place of Refuge, the perpetrator had to swim across the bay of shark-infested waters to reach the stone structure where the priests, or kahunas, received them for absolution.

After listening to the history of the place, we all group together in the amphitheatre to read the modern form of Ho'oponopono to our small class. A simplified version of this forgiveness prayer was brought to the western culture by Morrnah Nalamaku Simeona, a modern day Hawaiian Kahuna. Ho'oponopono means to set right, to re-establish order and balance in our thoughts, words, deeds, and actions. To do Ho'oponopono daily, even moment to moment, is to ask that our minds be cleansed of memories that are replaying in our experience as problems and errors. It is an invocation to Divinity to absolve us of these thoughts that are toxic and imbalanced, so we can walk in a sacred manner and have all of our thoughts and actions produce peace, love, order and balance.

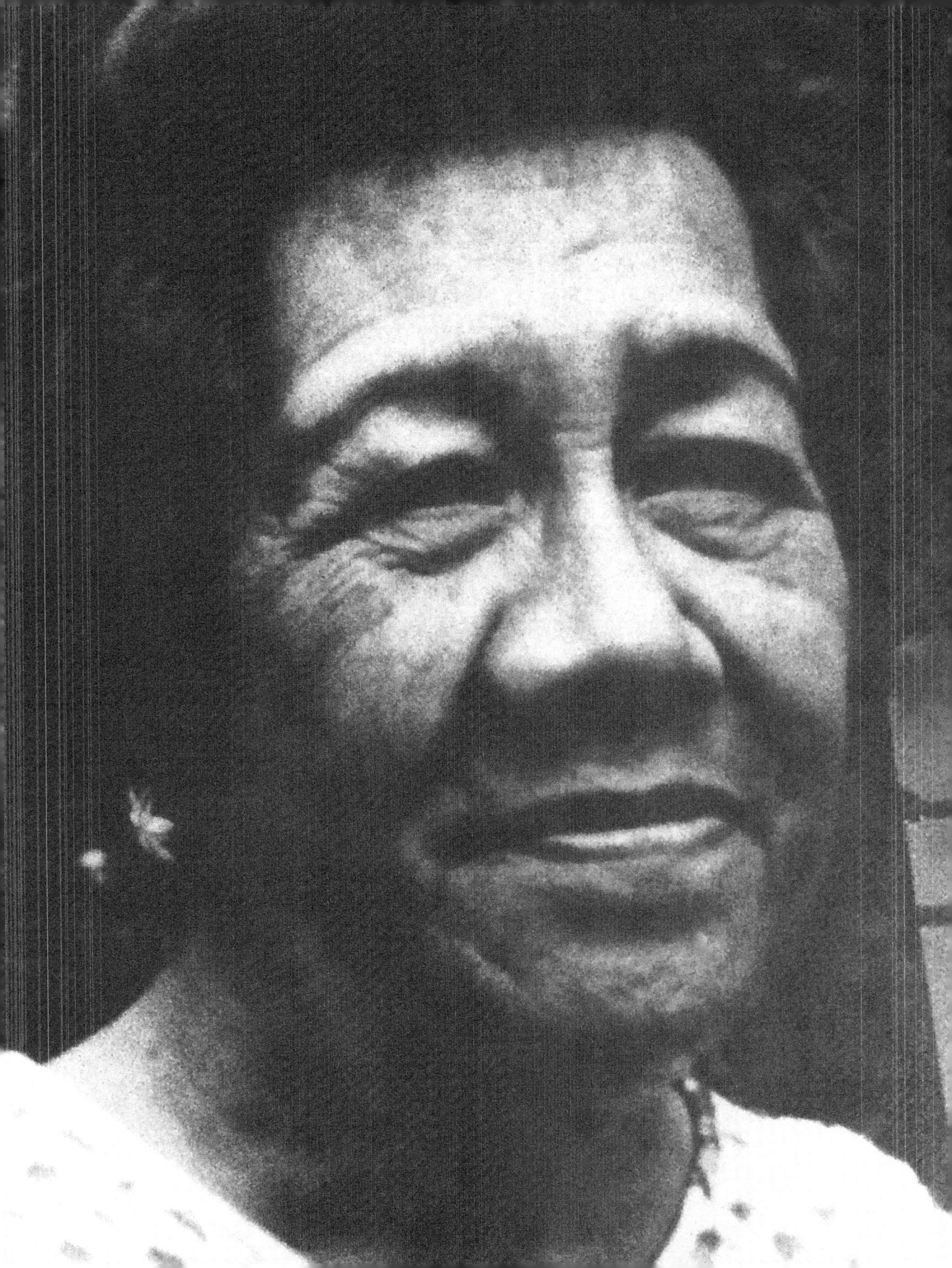

At the Pu'uhonua, we find ourselves at the place where Ho'oponopono makes the most sense historically. We sit to write down all the people, places, things and situations we would like to include in the process to be cleansed of our thought forms. As the group writes these down, we explain the breathing that will take place in two of the twelve steps. Ho'oponopono is in keeping with Liberation Breathing®, because the kahunas knew that breathing was a major element for their prayers to work. Also, including the subconscious mind in the prayer is essential. Pranayama, Liberation Breathing®, and the breathing in Ho'oponopono are very different in form, but their purpose is similar: to line up the subconscious mind, the conscious mind, and the super conscious mind so that the Life Force can fully flow through us in our life. This means our body, mind, and spirit are fully integrated and in balance, producing an experience of heaven on earth.

We read the Ho'oponopono to the group as we do the process on ourselves. Such a deep sense of satisfaction comes over me, that we are fulfilling our function as students and teachers. Our students participating in the Liberation Breathing Intensive are getting a full dose of the best Hawaii has to offer. We complete the twelve-step prayer and sit in the stillness of the cleansing. All feel the presence of grace as well as an extreme and pleasant exhaustion after a full morning and afternoon of spiritual attentiveness.

Part 5

Selecting or Becoming a Liberation Breathing Practitioner

What Makes a Good Liberation Breathing Practitioner

Select a practitioner for yourself by following your intuition. *Who do you feel safe with? Who do you trust?* Naturally, you have a right to ask about their training. At LiberationBreathing.com we offer you a list of certified LB® Practitioners. It is my experience that a good practitioner is someone who has the following:

- love of God
- love of life
- love of others
- love of self
- love of the process itself
- proper training (as mentioned earlier)
- a high level of intuition

LB® practitioners should know:

- basic metaphysics
- birth and relationships data
- technology of the breath
- spiritual clarity
- spiritual healing
- physical immortality and ascension
- relationships technology (basics of Loving Relationships Training®)
- conflict resolution
- counseling skills
- fundamentals of medicine and psychology
- fundamentals of addiction/co-dependency
- interviewing techniques

As far as I am concerned a LB® practitioner needs to be in training for life! Every moment everywhere with every person should be used as a training ground to become better and clearer in supporting clients.

Specifically, LB® practitioners should possess:
- self esteem
- certainty
- organizing skills
- public speaking skills
- confidence in using their intuition
- prosperity/money skills
- a self-employment training skill set
- a global perspective
- clarity on service to humanity
- prayers and mantras relating to the Divine Mother

The qualities of a good LB® practitioner are:
- loving
- patient
- clear
- secure
- intuitive
- centered
- present
- able to set their own case aside
- calm in all situations
- aligned with codes of ethics

It has been our experience that an ordinary housewife who is pure and loving may make a better LB® practitioner than a person with a lot of degrees. The former is usually in her heart chakra and the latter might be stuck in the head. What really makes a good practitioner is someone who has worked out his or her own birth-death cycle. That *release* makes all the difference in the world, because a telepathic space is made available wherein the client can surrender his or her own birth-death cycle. The client feels safe with a practitioner who is free of anger and fear.

If the practitioner is clear (subconscious baggage has been released), her intuition is more accurate and she instinctively knows what to do, what to say, and how to be in a session. If her own case is in the way, her natural intuition is blocked. Until we are all like Jesus and Babaji we have something to clear, so it is not expected that a practitioner is 100 percent at the level of Jesus (*wouldn't that be nice?*). The main point is that practitioners can put their own case aside (on the shelf so to speak) and be totally present. Even more important is that he or she realize that God is acting through them, and that they need to "get out of the way."

All good LB® practitioners should know how to process themselves. The more they know how to process themselves, the better they will be at processing the client. All LB® practitioners absolutely need to have regular sessions themselves by a more qualified practitioner. This is a life-long process. In other words, every LB® practitioner needs a LB® practitioner of his own, and that is absolutely mandatory. It is not acceptable if a LB® practitioner or a rebirther stops getting sessions by a peer at the same level or higher.

This is a life-long path. One does not have to be perfect to be a practitioner, but one has to be two steps ahead of the client. There is a danger when a practitioner thinks he knows it all or does not need any more trainings or updates. But the biggest mistake of all is to think that as a practitioner one does not need to have breathing sessions any longer. It is totally appropriate for a client to ask, "And who is *your* practitioner or rebirther?"

We recommend that a Liberation Breathing® practitioner should have sessions with a more experienced practitioner at least once or twice per month. If they love breathing, they would love to do that—period! This can be worked out for pay or trade. While practitioners can breathe themselves, it is not the same as having a facilitated session with a more skilled practitioner. In this way you can go deeper and face issues commonly avoided when breathing by oneself.

Liberation Breathing® is an art and a science. Just to keep up on the latest research is not enough. We need to become as professional as possible, while maintaining the uniqueness of our understanding of surrender to God and lack of form. Instead of just taking trainings, all practitioners need to surrender to each other's knowledge from experience, which must be shared. The ego is tricky. A practitioner may need to be cleared by another just when they think they don't need it. Checks and balances are important. I have found it immensely valuable to throw myself at the feet of other skilled practitioners who would nail me on my case and not be willing to put up with escape mechanisms. I use peer reviews frequently. This is the main reason I go to India every year—to get blasted by the saints and masters. I literally beg them to correct me on anything. The short amount of agony that one might go through getting processed by a spiritual master is nothing compared to the long-term agony of dragging out one's case in front of the world.

Training for the Liberation Breathing Practitioner

Since Markus and I were entrusted with Liberation Breathing®, which includes maintaining its integrity, we have identified what we believe is the proper training for a practitioner of this beautiful work. A LB® practitioner is required to:

- receive 10 sessions by a professional female LB® Practitioner or rebirther (to clear "mother issues")
- receive 10 sessions by a professional male LB® Practitioner or rebirther (to clear "father issues")
- take The Loving Relationships Training®
- take Liberation Breathing Intensive Part I (6-day seminar; schedule available at LiberationBreathing.com)
- take Liberation Breathing Intensive Part II wet training in thermal waters (6-day seminar; schedule available at LiberationBreathing.com)
- continually and daily study *A Course in Miracles*, sourced from the Christ Mind
- Facilitate ten LB® sessions for two female clients and two male clients
- provide case studies while in training to the Liberation Breathing® Body (visit LiberationBreathing.com for detailed guidelines)
- master the checklist of birth types that practitioners should know regarding how birth affects relationships

- take the Hawaiian forgiveness process called Ho'oponopono; use it daily
- surrender to the Divine Mother and incorporate honoring Her daily in some form of worship. (We read the 108 names and praises to the Divine Mother each morning.) This daily worship is essential.
- surrender to Babaji, the father of Liberation Breathing®
- attend the Divine Mother Navaratri in India or at another one of Babaji's ashrams around the world (details available at LiberationBreathing.com)
- be willing to meet with Ammachi, the Divine Mother in physical form
- commit to training for life
- become licensed through the Liberation Breathing® Body
- take a refresher Liberation Breathing® course once a year to stay current
- schedule Liberation Breathing® or rebirthing sessions for yourself from a qualified practitioner regularly (at least 1-2 per month)
- handle assignments specific to your own personal case
- organize one workshop per year for LiberationBreathing.com
- be actively involved with the Liberation Breathing® network

Note: It certainly is not necessary that a person who does Liberation Breathing® become a Babaji devotee. However, we feel practitioners must be open to His guidance and energy field to stay as clear and as skilled as possible. Babaji is always blessing this work and he has always protected our clients.

A Checklist for Liberation Breathing Practitioners and Clients

Step 1: Complete ten or more Liberation Breathing® sessions with a trained practitioner of your choice. (Do not jump from one practitioner to another in the beginning.) The sessions are intuitive and gentle; the breathing is connected, rhythmical, and deep in the upper chest. Going for drama or "acting out" instead of going for the release through breathing can require a lot more sessions. A relaxed, intuitive breathing rhythm is the key. By this time you should have thoroughly exposed yourself to the philosophy of physical immortality and the psychology of unraveling the personal death urge, although this will be an ongoing process.

Step 2: Choose a practitioner of the opposite sex now. If you started with a woman, switch to a man or vice versa. This will activate different material. You should now read the appropriate books to facilitate your process, attend seminars, and know what support from a spiritual family and community means.

Step 3: Start wet Liberation Breathing® in warm water (approximately 103°F). Get yourself a good nose plug and sturdy snorkel shaped in a J. (I personally don't like the kind with the blow hole.) Get your swimsuit and towel, and in the water roll up in the fetal position and follow what your practitioner says. You should maintain the breathing rhythm that you have mastered. Do NOT try this on your own until your practitioner says you are ready.

Step 4: Cold water Liberation Breathing® supports the release of anesthesia and the death urge. Leonard Orr likes to go in slowly, putting one foot in while maintaining breathing and move in an inch at a time, while maintaining breathing. I can't handle that way myself. I prefer to go straight in all the way. It is up to you and your practitioner.

Step 5: Master spiritual healing and begin to rebirth yourself when your practitioner says you are ready.

Note: Even after you learn all aspects of Liberation Breathing® and you can take yourself through a full breathing cycle, you should always schedule sessions with a qualified LB® practitioner from time to time. The sharing is an integral part of the process, and requires two people. Liberation Breathing® is a life-long spiritual path that you will want to practice frequently, if not daily.

Part 6

The Power of Processing Thoughts

The Purity of Liberation Breathing

One of the biggest goals of Liberation Breathing® is to release people from *suppressed* guilt and get them in touch with the inner purity and innocence of their real Self. We have extracted statements that *A Course in Miracles* makes about purity below. Seeing through the eyes of purity is the real key. The purpose of Liberation Breathing® is to give us *Holy vision*, free of all guilt, to the Self of our total innocence—what Jesus says is our true Identity.

As Liberation Breathing® practitioners it is our job to see our clients' purity and help them release everything that keeps them from experiencing this purity. Lesson 263 in *A Course in Miracles* teaches: "My holy vision sees all things as pure." When we first see ourselves as pure, we create the vibration of purity. Both the breathing itself and the client must be viewed as pure for the session to be completely pure. In this purity the client is liberated from guilt, the great destroyer of life itself. *A Course in Miracles* repeatedly says that we believe we are guilty because we think we separated from God and we made this separation real. Until we heal our guilt we will never be liberated.

Death is an ultimate punishment to ourselves, since we believe we are sinners for being separate. *A Course in Miracles* unravels our guilt (ego) and Jesus does it step by step by giving us this curriculum. Liberation Breathing® goes hand in hand with *A Course in Miracles* because we let go of the guilt through the breath. The more we breathe guilt out, the more we can integrate what *A Course in Miracles* has to teach us. We are so grateful these two offerings came to the planet about the same time.

Teachings on Purity from A Course in Miracles

"For the Son of God is guiltless now, and the brightness of his purity shines untouched forever in God." T13 I. 5:6

"By accepting his purity as yours, learn of him that it *is* ours." T13 I. 7:6

"Thus does the Son of God give thanks unto his Father for his purity." T13 VII. 17:9

"In shining peace within you is the perfect purity in which you were created." T13 X. 9:4

"He would show you the perfect purity that is forever within God's Son." T13 X. 10:11

"Behold the Son of God and look upon his purity and be still." T13 X. 11:10

"His shining purity, wholly untouched by guilt and wholly loving, is bright within you." T13 X. 12:2

"I thank You, Father, for the purity of Your most holy Son, whom You have created guiltless forever." T13 X. 12:6

"Nothing can shake God's conviction of the perfect purity of everything that He created, for it *is* wholly pure." T14 III. 12:2

"The Holy Spirit knows that all salvation is escape from guilt. You have no other 'enemy,' and against this strange distortion of the purity of the Son of God the Holy Spirit is your only Friend." T14 III.13:4-5

"There is nothing in the Mind of God that does not share His shining innocence. Creation is a natural extension of perfect purity. Your only calling here is to devote yourself, with active willingness, to the denial of guilt in all forms." T14 V. 3:3-5

"Protect his purity from every thought that would steal it away and keep it from his sight." T14 V. 4:3

"Never allow purity to remain hidden, but shine away the heavy veils of guilt within which the Son of God has hidden himself from his own sight. T14 V. 4:5

"Peace is the acknowledgement of perfect purity, from which no one is excluded. T14 V. 8:2

"Each one you see you place within the holy circle of Atonement or leave outside, judging him fit for crucifixion or for redemption. If you bring him into the circle of purity, you will rest there with him." T14 V. 11:1-2

"In the temple, Holiness waits quietly for the return of them that love it. The Presence knows they will return to purity and to grace. T14 IX. 4:1-2

"There never was an instant where God's Son could lose his purity." T15 I. 15:5

"His changeless state is beyond time, for his purity remains forever beyond attack and without variability." T15 I. 15:6

"Let the Holy Spirit's purity shine them away, and bring all your awareness to the readiness for purity He offers you." T15 IV. 9:9

"This world of light, this circle of brightness, is the real world where guilt meets with forgiveness…. Here are the dark and heavy garments of guilt laid by, and gently replaced by purity and love." T18 IX. 9:1,7

"A major tenet in the ego's insane religion is that sin is not error but truth. Purity is seen as arrogance, and the acceptance of the self as sinful is perceived as holiness. T19 II. 4:1-2

"This [Holy] week we celebrate life not death. And we honor the perfect purity of the Son of God, and not his sins." T20 I. 2:3-4

"And as you look upon your brother, you will see an altar to your Father, holy as Heaven, glowing with radiant purity and sparkling with shining lilies you laid upon it." T20 VIII. 4:4

"Heaven is the home of perfect purity, and God created it for you. Look on your holy brother sinless as yourself and let him lead you there." T22 II. 13:6-7

"Love must be extended. Purity is not confined. It is the nature of the innocent to be forever uncontained, without a barrier or limitation." T28 II. 2:1-3

"Christ's vision beholds a light beyond the body; an idea beyond what can be touched; a purity undimmed by errors, pitiful mistakes and fearful thoughts of guilt and dreams of sin." WB Lesson 158 7:3

"The Son of God is My Identity. My Self is holy beyond all the thoughts of holiness of which I now conceive, its shimmering and perfect purity is far more brilliant than is any light that I have ever looked upon." WB Lesson 252 1:1-2

"My holy vision sees all things as pure. A madman's dream is hardly fit to be my choice, instead of all the loveliness with which you blessed creation; all its purity, its joy and its eternal, quiet home in you." WB Lesson 263 1:4

When Jesus says, "Christ's vision beholds a light beyond the body; an idea beyond what can be touched; a purity undimmed by errors, pitiful mistakes and fearful thoughts of guilt and dreams of sin," He is asking us to see ourselves and others with the vision of the forgiven world. He is asking us, as breathworkers and sane human beings, to set aside our judgments and see with "eyes of purity." *Are you willing to drop your judgments and conflicts for a vision of peace and joy?* We are capable of having this vision when we give attention to inner correction, inner forgiveness, and letting go of the past. It is a vision beyond the "body's eyes" of perception. It is rather a "spiritual sight" in which the oneness of relationships is respected and honored. In this way of seeing, the lessons of *A Course in Miracles* coupled with the practice of Liberation Breathing® are catalysts to having this inner vision of wholeness and purity. Listen to our dialogue on the "vision of purity" at MiraclesArePresent.com.

Affirmations

An affirmation is a positive thought that you choose to integrate into your consciousness to produce a new desired result. It is used repetitiously until the desired result is manifested. Your mind will create whatever you want it to, if you give it a chance. The subconscious mind can be impressed like a piece of clay. We always give clients personalized affirmations to write after each private Liberation Breathing® session, depending on what comes up in that session.

There are various ways to use affirmations. A simple and effective way to use affirmations is to write each affirmation 10-20 times on the left side of a sheet of paper, leaving a space on the right margin for responses of the mind or emotional reactions. Jot down on the right side of the page whatever thoughts, considerations, beliefs, fears, or emotions that may come into your mind in opposition to your affirmation. Continue writing the affirmation and observe how the responses on the right side change. A powerful affirmation will bring up all the negative thoughts and feelings stored deep in your consciousness and you will have the opportunity to discover what is standing between you and your goal. Affirmations are not just "glossing things over." The repetitive use of an affirmation will impress upon your mind and simultaneously erase the old thought pattern, producing permanent desirable changes in your life!

Thoughts produce results. Be sure that you are willing to take on the added responsibilities, new adventure, and challenges that will manifest as a result of breaking the old mold. It is helpful and powerful to experience the feeling and the visualization of the affirmation as you say it or write it. Remember, affirmations are very powerful and need to be carefully worded.

Making Affirmations Work for You

1. Work with one or more every day. The best times are just before sleeping, before starting the day, and especially whenever you feel depressed or discouraged.
2. Write each affirmation 10-20 times.

3. Insert your name. Say or write each affirmation in the first, second, and third person. Writing in the second and third person is important since your conditioning from others came to you in this manner.

   - "I, _____, am increasing my willingness to be loved."
   - "You, _____, are increasing your willingness to be loved."
   - "She/he, _____, is increasing her willingness to be loved."

4. Continue working with the affirmations daily until they become totally integrated into your consciousness. You will know this when your mind responds positively and you begin to experience new intended results.
5. Saying the affirmations aloud also works. Repeat them regularly on schedule. For instance, five minutes in the morning, noon, and at night for seven days.
6. Record your affirmations on a digital recorder and play them back whenever you can. Speak each affirmation ten times (slowly) into the recorder so you have time to think about them between each one. Replay when you are driving or when you go to bed.
7. Look in the mirror and say your affirmations out loud to yourself, even if you feel silly. Continue until you are able to experience yourself with a relaxed happy expression at all times—eliminating all facial tension and grimaces.
8. Sit across from a friend, each of you in a straight-back chair with your hands on your thighs and knees barely touching each other. Say the affirmation to your friend until you are comfortable doing so. Then have him or her say it to you in the second person. Ask your partner to observe your body language carefully: if you squirm, fidget, or are messing around, continue with the same affirmation. Do not move on to a new affirmation until you say the first one clearly and can receive it clearly back.
9. It is also effective to type affirmations. However, an advantage to writing is that you can observe your handwriting changes as emotions come up! They seem to go deeper by writing in long hand. If you are

writing affirmations, it is a good idea to stop using the response column after a week in order to avoid indulging in negatives that come up. You could then switch to a digital recording.

10. As you read over the sample affirmations included here, note which ones have the greatest emotional reaction (charge) for you and mark them. Those that bring up the most resistance are the ones to do! Work on no more than three per week. Then, let go and let them sink into your subconscious.

Self Esteem Affirmations

Insert your name in the blank.

I, _____, like myself. I am a lovable person.

I, _____, am highly pleasing to myself.

I, _____, am now highly pleasing to myself in the presence of other people.

I, _____, am highly pleasing to others and others are highly pleasing to me.

I, _____, am a self-determined person, and I allow others the same right.

I, _____, have the right to say no to people without losing their love.

Other people have the right to say no to me without hurting me.

I, _____, like myself, therefore I like others.

I, _____, like myself, therefore others like me.

I, _____, like others, therefore others like me.

The more I like myself, the more others like themselves in my presence.

I, _____, am attractive and lovable. The more I acknowledge that, the truer it becomes.

My defense mechanisms are no longer necessary because I am a wonderful person.

The more I enjoy being alone, the more I enjoy being with others.

I, _____, am loved and appreciated whether I am with someone or not.

Enlightenment through the Holy Spirit's Thought System

One purpose of Liberation Breathing® is to help you become as enlightened as possible. Before *A Course in Miracles* became available, a standard definition of enlightenment was attaining certain knowledge of the Absolute Truth—the one and only truth that is true throughout all time and space for everyone. *What is the absolute truth?* The truth is: "The thinker is creative with his thoughts." The Bible affirms it saying, "For as he thinketh in his heart, so is he." (Prov 23:7, KJV)

Your thoughts *always* produce results. *Are you thinking negative thoughts that give you negative results? Or, are you thinking positive thoughts that give you positive results?* In order to get positive results in your life all the time, convert your negative thoughts into positive thoughts. Change your feelings in this same way, since feelings are structures of thought. *How do you handle the unconscious thoughts that are producing results you don't want?* First, become aware of the thoughts in your subconscious! This is where Liberation Breathing® comes in. When you breathe in this circular smooth rhythm, your unconscious comes to your conscious awareness without drugs or hypnosis. Here are the principles of how the mind works:

- You create your own reality—every part of it. You create it through your own beliefs, expectations, attitudes, desires, fears, judgments, interpretations, feelings, and especially persistent thoughts.
- You get what you concentrate on.
- You even get what you do not concentrate on from your subconscious thoughts.
- You are 100 percent responsible for your own experience.
- Thoughts will telepathically attract their equivalent. Positive thoughts will attract positive people, positive things, and positive results; negative thoughts will attract negative people, negative things, and negative results.
- Life presents to you what your thoughts are.
- As you change your thoughts you change your experience.

- You are unlimited. There are no boundaries. The Thought of God is infinite and unlimited; therefore, everything that exists is unlimited. You are part of the Mind of God; therefore, all you have to do is believe it. When thinking with God, anything is possible.
- The present is the fruit of the past and the seed of the future.
- The world is what you think it is. You can change your world by changing your thoughts. Energy flows wherever your attention goes.
- Nothing ever happens to you without you calling for it, or without your participation (when a bad result occurs, it is usually attracted unconsciously).
- You create exactly what your vibe is.
- Think about what you *want* because you are going to get what you think.
- The mind rules the body. The body is at the effect of the mind.
- Negative thoughts produce negative results in the body.
- All illness is mental illness. The physician is the mind of the patient himself. (*A Course in Miracles*)
- You are not a victim. There are no victims. *A Course in Miracles* says, "Beware of the temptation to perceive yourself as unfairly treated."
- Everything in our life—every experience, every relationship—is a mirror of the mental patterns going on inside us.

A Course in Miracles has an ever higher definition of enlightenment: "You are enlightened when you trade in the ego's thought system for the Holy Spirit's thought system." This is the result we are going for in Liberation Breathing®. *What does A Course in Miracles mean by that?* The ego's thought system is based on the thought, "I am separate from God." This makes us feel like a sinner and we get the thought, "I am a sinner." This leads to guilt. Guilt leads to fear because guilt demands punishment. Fear leads to pain. Pain leads to anger, misery, conflict, suffering, poor health, aging, and death. Death is a result of the thought called the ego. This, according to *A Course in Miracles*, is the descent into hell. Hell is what the ego makes of the present.

The Holy Spirit's mind is our *true* reality. There is no separation between you and God. There is no guilt; therefore, we are innocent. If we are innocent, we can have love, peace, joy, harmony, happiness, relaxation, perfect health, and longevity. It is our job to trade in the former (ego's thought system) for the latter (Holy Spirit's thought system). *Who would not want the latter?* We must, however, give up our addiction to the ego (our collection of negative thoughts). *A Course in Miracles* is a correction of religion. The *Course* says, "This is a required course." My experience is that the more Liberation Breathing® I do, the more I can let in *A Course in Miracles* and the more I can replace the ego with the Holy Spirit. In this way, Liberation Breathing® leads to enlightenment as the *Course* defines it.

The greatest gift you can offer the world, yourself, and your children is a clear consciousness, free of distracting or sabotaging thoughts. A well-trained LB® practitioner can help you identify even preverbal thoughts that trace back to your birth or the womb. You would be surprised what sophisticated thoughts a baby can have. These preverbal thoughts are unconscious. Once we remove negative unconscious material from our minds, our whole life can change. A LB® practitioner helps you raise the quality of your thoughts and speech.

Verbal Processing

One of the big contributions I originally made to rebirthing is the art of verbal processing, a form of self-inquiry. It is essential to know where you are stuck and to be able to do something about it by breathing and changing your thoughts. One definition of a humble person is that he is willing to recognize his errors, admit them, *and* do something about them. Through processing, one can learn to recognize errors that may be hidden.

Why do it? My colleague Leslie Temple Thurston in her book *The Marriage of Spirit* covers this question very well. She says that when we process, we inquire deeply into the nature of our conditioned and unbalanced ego patterning with the intention of finding the truth. With her permission, I summarize her points below. Thurston indicates that processing helps us:

- find out who we are.
- become more aware, flexible, and free.
- function to the best of our ability.
- cope with the speed of our evolution.
- let go of obsolete teachings from childhood.
- become free of the past while bringing clarity to future goals.
- let go of extraneous baggage while maximizing time in an overextended world.
- cope with life's challenges.
- have resources for insight and creativity.

Thurston says, "A cleared consciousness is the most valuable asset to life!"

Verbal processing with a client before the breath cycle in a Liberation Breathing® session makes breathing go easier. The negative thoughts are exposed, loosened up, and come out of the cells more quickly. When you create an unpleasant experience, you have to look at it and clear it. You can say, "I will not do *that* again." But old programs keep replaying. Erasing the old program is key. You can do this by processing to become aware of the program and then breathe it out. Untie the knots in your mind. This will happen with the breathing alone. *Breathing itself is a form of processing. By verbal processing first, it all goes faster.* It is great to get the "a-hah" when you reveal hidden patterns, and this also gives you a deeper connection with your soul.

Processing shifts your consciousness and therefore it shifts your body. Liberation Breathing® always shifts the body, which is why I love it so much. I do feel it is important to choose a practitioner who is good at processing. *Who wants to keep living in the same old situations?* Most people rerun the same patterns their entire lives without realizing how this weakens them. It slows down your vibrational frequency tremendously. Processing ourselves out of unbalanced states of mind speeds up our vibrational frequency and gives more inner strength.

The Ultimate Truth Process for Self-Healing

"The Ultimate Truth Process" is an important aspect of verbal processing that I developed several years ago through extensive meditation, prayer, and study of *A Course in Miracles*. I teach it to all LB® practitioners. Any time you have a negative symptom in your body, be it as minor as a headache or a disease as serious as cancer, you can begin clearing it immediately in the following manner. Take out a notebook or three sheets of paper and write at the top (using front and back):

The reasons I have this condition are:

> *Keep writing all the reasons until they begin to repeat themselves. They will come out as negative thoughts. Some of them may sound ridiculous. Put them down anyway.*

My "payoffs" for having this condition are:

> *A payoff is a negative, neurotic reinforcement of something you are getting to prove. What do I get to prove by having this condition?*

My fears of giving up this condition are:

> *You may not think you are afraid of giving it up. If you weren't you would have already let go of it. Many are afraid of the newfound energy they will experience without the condition.*

My most negative thought about myself is:

> *Write down your most negative thought about yourself, your life, and your body. These thoughts plus the other negative thoughts you have written down in the exercise are causing your condition or disease. Negative thoughts actually create what we call "negative mental mass" which cause physical symptoms.*

The main reason I do not want to give up this condition is:

Take note of what was happening in your life the first time you ever got this condition. What was the triggering factor? The deepest reason may be wired to a "survival script"—an incorrect belief that without the thought, action, or condition you will die.

My new affirmation from this exercise is:

Transform the negative thoughts that came up to positive affirmations and work with them daily.

Schedule with your LB® practitioner to breathe out these negative thoughts permanently from your body and to develop your new affirmations. This exercise can be used multiple times. Begin with your most challenging physical symptom. When you know the causative "thought factors" that are resulting in your condition, you are in a position to forgive and release these thoughts. You are able to breathe out these thoughts in session. You are able to heal yourself with your mind and the help of the Holy Spirit. This information is very important for your practitioner to have so they can process you efficiently.

Your thoughts produce results in your body and your body is "at the effect of" your mind. *A Course in Miracles* says, "All illness is mental illness and the physician is the mind of the patient himself." Once you accept this, you can heal yourself with your mind, by un-creating negative thoughts. Quite simply, once you locate the negative thoughts that created your symptom/disease, all you have to do is change those thoughts to the opposite and breathe out the old thoughts. Commitment on your part is essential. Changing a thought *once* that you have held for thirty years is not enough. The new affirmation must be repeated over and over in your mind until your mind is reprogrammed. The old thought must be breathed out of your cells and neutralized. It must be totally *forgiven*.

The conscious raising of your thoughts to higher thoughts and conscious breathing can produce permanent healing. I have seen people through breathing sessions heal themselves of cancer and all types of conditions. It is very common to see these miracles. Because I have certainty that anything can be healed and anything created can be uncreated, things happen fast in my presence.

Louise Hay Explains The Mental Causes of Physical Illness

Even after understanding how the mind itself creates disease, I began to wonder why in one patient the liver was affected, in another ulcers resulted, and in yet another skin eruptions occurred. *If it was all due to the mind, why were different parts of the body affected?* These questions haunted me. I was fortunate to have in one LRT® the great metaphysical healer Louise Hay who studied these questions. I was relieved when she gave me her wonderful little book *Heal Your Body* (newest edition *Heal Your Body A-Z*) It is just amazing.

Here are some examples:

Problem	Metaphysical Cause
Allergies	Who are you allergic to? Denying your own power.
Back problems	Lack of support.
Colds	Confusion, disorder, small hurts.
Diabetes	Deep sense of sorrow; no sweetness to life.
Eye problems	Not liking what you see in your own life. Fear of future.
Fatigue	Resistance. Boredom. Lack of love for what one does.
Knee problems	Inflexibility, fear, ego, pride, inability to bend.
Throat problems	Avenue of expression. Repressed anger. Emotional hurt swallowed.

The whole book made sense to me, so I started carrying it everywhere and telling people to get it. I encourage you to read it!

Processing the Fear of Giving Up an Addiction

Let's say you repeat the same old bothersome behavior over and over. You yourself are annoyed with it and probably your mate is also. But you cannot seem to stop it by your will. Time to go to a Liberation Breathing® practitioner! In the session you will recognize this not only as a pattern, but probably as a mental addiction.

Thoughts and patterns become addictive. Your ego loves to keep you stuck. After much study, what I discovered about addictions is that in order to let them go, you have to process the fear of giving them up. (I had to read *A Course in Miracles* four times before I figured this out.) Let's say I have a habit of overspending. I know it is not good, but I keep doing it. My practitioner, properly trained, would ask me to repeat the following out loud:

- My fear of giving up this addiction is _____.
- Another fear I have of giving up this addiction forever is _____.

Then I have to process the fear. Let's say my fear is that if I don't overspend, I will keep the money and then something terrible will happen if people find out I have money. This could be due to a past life where I was rich and something happened that was dangerous, i.e., I was killed because I was rich. So in this life I have to get rid of money quickly. The final step is to change that thought (reverse into a positive thought or affirmation) and breathe out the fear.

Let's say I go to a practitioner because I have a problem with someone. The best thing is to get myself processed first and get out of blame. I need to get processed on my part of the situation and I need to breathe and open my heart first before having a confrontation with the other person. If I suppress it all and don't get processed and don't do the breathing, it might make me end up like a pressure cooker and that is not good for my health.

The LB® practitioner processes with the following question types:

- What does this remind you of in your past?
- The reason I created this situation was _____.
- What I need to let go of in myself to clear this is _____.

Then I lie down and breathe it out. The phrase "I don't know," is not a final answer. That is just my unwillingness to be free of the negative pattern. When a client is uncertain or "doesn't know" an answer, The LB® practitioner says:
- If you did know the cause, what would it be?

Uncovering the Personal Lie

Now you are ready to find out one of the most important things Liberation Breathing® has to offer—getting rid of your *personal lie*. Until this is discovered and released one cannot reach full potential. You may be doing great, but you will become a lot greater after you uncover this one. After you start breathing consciously you will eventually get in touch with your personal lie—your most dominant negative consciousness factor or core belief about yourself. It is the one main thought that is the major block to your happiness and aliveness. It is *not* a truth, even though your experience may attest otherwise. A good LB® practitioner is able to crack this one in the first session. Until you get rid of it, life can be hard. Your personal lie is the cornerstone of the ego (a collection of limiting, negative thoughts that keep you from remembering you are one with God). You probably had it since birth or before. Perhaps you even had it several lifetimes back. Worse still, your ego tricks you into proving that it is right! Most are addicted to the thought without even knowing it.

Here are some of the common personal lies we find buried in the subconscious of clients:
- I am not good enough.
- I am bad.
- I am wrong.
- I am not perfect.
- I am weak.
- I am guilty.
- I can't.
- I can't make it.
- I am not capable.

- I am a failure.
- Something is wrong with me.
- I am a disappointment.
- I shouldn't be here.
- I am unwanted.
- I am evil.
- I am stuck.
- I am nothing.
- I don't matter.
- I am a burden.
- I hurt people.
- I am a fake.
- I am an imposter.
- I ruin things.
- I am a killer.

Some of these thoughts relate directly to the birth script. *I am unwanted* is a conception trauma of someone who was not wanted by one or both parents. *I am a disappointment* is often a thought of someone born to parents who wanted the opposite sex. *I am a killer* could derive from a past life or a belief that one's mother was dying during childbirth.

In Liberation Breathing® sessions and seminars, we uncover the predominant negative thought held by each individual. It is imperative to get down to the exact right thought for yourself. It is crucial to see how this negative, sabotaging thought is affecting your life! Because of your personal lie (which you subconsciously *bought into* somewhere along the line), you create situations to prove it is so, thus reinforcing the belief. For example, if your personal lie is "I am not good enough," you will unconsciously set up situations in which you look or feel not good enough. You will go after these situations or make them up to attempt to prove the *truth* of your personal lie. You will come out looking and feeling not good enough and then you will say to yourself, "This *proves* I am not good enough." The only way out of this trap is to isolate your personal lie and transcend it absolutely. It affects the cells. It has to be reversed *and* breathed out.

Simply saying "I *am* good enough" a few times will not do the trick. You most likely won't believe your affirmation, since you have indulged in your personal lie for years. You have to start convincing yourself of the new thought by repetition and by getting the old thought out of the cells through conscious breathing. You need a constant diet of forgiveness to release yourself from the consequences of thinking your personal lie is true.

There is likely to be resistance to giving up this thought completely, because your whole life has been about proving it, wrestling with it, and working around it. When it goes, there will be the death of that part of your mind and your whole reality will change. Some people are so afraid of change that they would rather hang on to what was familiar and die than leap into a new reality that would bring about more life. Sometimes we are also afraid to change because our birth was a big change from liquid to air, and we got hurt in the process. Fear comes because it would be unfamiliar *not* to have that thought about yourself, and people are often afraid of the unfamiliar.

I assure you that life will not only be better without hanging on to the personal lie, it will be heaven. Ask God's help to give it up. Release any fears of heaven consciousness and of having more fun. Be vigilant against the ego. The ego is going to trick you into thinking it is better to hang on to the thought and remain stuck.

Some fear the tremendous increase in energy resulting in giving up the personal lie. It is true—you will have increased energy. If you are afraid of energy, release these fears, including any fear of the Holy Spirit (energy).

A person's tendency is to do one of the following things with their personal lie:
- act it out
- suppress it and overcompensate
- project it onto others

For example, people with the personal lie "I am bad" may act bad and do things that are bad, bringing on themselves judgment from others and actually reinforcing the thought of badness. Or they may work very hard to keep the thought of being bad completely hidden from other people and act really, really good all of the time; but it comes out like being a fake. It is a cover-up. Or finally, they may project "I am bad" onto others and see everyone else as bad. Their mate is bad, their boss is bad, their neighbors are bad, and so on. It is important to know the personal lie of your mate if you want your relationship to work.

One thing we have to deal with as practitioners is the following: Having survived both birth and infancy with the personal lie, the person suffers an unconscious fear that he or she will die if he or she gives up the thought. This thought has actually become a *survival script*. Of course this does not make any sense. It is just a trick of the ego. Some people think that once they discover this thought they can just drop it overnight. Our experience is different. People usually have too much fear of that much light entering all at once. It would be too much energy to handle all at once. So they seem to chip away at it. All of this fear can be breathed out in a Liberation Breathing® session on the exhale!

In my book *Healing and Holiness*, I detail how personal lies can interfere with healing the body, negative patterns, or relationships. Here are some examples:

I am not good enough. This person may hold the thought "I am not good enough to be healed." No matter how many healing opportunities are given, none will help because deep down those with this thought believe they are not good enough to deserve the good result of healing. Tendency to create a sabotage pattern.

I am wrong. People who think they are wrong also think they deserve punishment. Illness or a failure of any kind may be the very punishment they think they deserve. These people may also attract the wrong diagnosis, the wrong medicine, the wrong doctor or healer, or the wrong partner for that matter. They may even get stuck on working on the wrong part of their mind, so they get nowhere.

I am not perfect. These people often make up little things wrong with their bodies or relationships so they can feel imperfect. They might be absolutely obsessed with the imperfections they create. As soon as they heal one imperfection in their life they make up another one so they can make sure they are never perfect. Even if they do find the right doctor or healer or breathing practitioner, they might set up their session to have something go wrong so they can prove the practitioner is imperfect.

I am guilty. Because guilt demands punishment, this person makes sure he or she is punished somehow. Example: They might become sexually promiscuous so they can continue the guilt cycle and come up with a sexually transmitted disease for a punishment. They may punish themselves in a number of ways, i.e., losing money, friends, or a good job to anything else that feeds the guilt and causes them to suffer. One of the common ways people act out the guilt is physical disease or in financial losses.

I can't or *I can't make it.* Sometimes these people create mysterious illnesses or diseases that cannot be diagnosed. They think they cannot heal themselves or be healed. Thoughts of helplessness and despair get stretched out to "I can't let go," "I can't get what I want," "I can't get rid of this condition." The worst is, "I can't let go of the thought I can't." They may have trouble at work doing a new task because of the thought "I can't." Many people with the personal lie "I can't make it," stay in relationships long after they are dead because they think they cannot make it on their own.

I am a failure. Imagine a person trying to heal him or herself of any condition (physical or emotional) with this thought. It won't work. They have set themselves up to fail at self-healing, relationships, and/or career. This could get so bad that it brings up the death urge and they want to check out. The conditions then get worse fast.

Something is wrong with me. This personal lie is a sure bet that something wrong will be created in the body. For example, I have known women with fertility problems who had the something-is-wrong-with-me syndrome. They ran from doctor to doctor to get proof of their infertility (which proved something was wrong with them). What they did not *get* was that their infertility problem itself was due to their personal lie!

I shouldn't be here. This personal lie can be deadly because these people have quite a death urge and may go around creating near fatal accidents and illnesses. More often than not, they live on the edge of personal disaster. They may go around bragging to others about how many near misses with death they have had. They may have a lot of out-of-body experiences, and might even make good clairvoyants, but it may be hard to keep them on this plane.

I am unwanted. People with this thought pattern are often attracted to people of the opposite sex who are not attracted to them so they can feel unwanted. The sadness of constant rejection can make them feel devastated and sick. They often cannot ask for the help they need because they think others do not want to help them. They may marry the first person that comes along to ask their hand even if they are not in love because they think nobody else would want them.

Although these negative thought patterns may seem rather extreme, the truth is that these patterns are more common that most people realize. We see them day in and day out. For decades I have watched people wrestle with these deep-rooted thoughts and their effects. Practitioners themselves have gone through their own personal lies and have a lot of compassion for this process. They know that on the other side of these thoughts is a whole new life. We have identified over 250 different personal lies so far. It is very important to find out yours with the exact wording. Your LB® practitioner knows how to do that.

Note: You could be one of the best healers in the world (and if you are, I salute you and hope to meet you), but all of your work with a client can go down the drain if the person goes back to his or her addictions and personal lies. For your work to have more lasting or permanent effects, please consider suggesting Liberation Breathing® to your clients to crack their case. They will appreciate you all the more, and your healing service will be more valuable in the end. Please consider this work for yourself also as your own healing abilities will greatly improve after you discover your own birth thoughts. If you get good results now, imagine what you might get after eliminating your own personal lie.

Processing Heavy Emotions

If you ever take the time to study the works of David Hawkins who wrote *Power vs. Force* and other marvelous books, you will find out that everyone has a specific calibrated level of consciousness at birth. This makes total sense based on our past life training. Unconditional love is calibrated at the level of 540. Enlightenment calibrates at 700-1,000. The problem we face in society is that 78 percent of the world population calibrates below level 200 (barely at the level of integrity), and that figure is only 49 percent in America (*Transcending the Levels of Consciousness, p. 29*).

That means most of the world is still dominated by primitive animal instincts, according to Hawkins. The brain's physiology changes dramatically at a consciousness level of 200. The quality of life changes and levels of power begin, rather than force. So look how far we have to go! In his brilliant book *Transcending the Levels of Consciousness* he rates the lower emotions:
- Shame is 20 points
- Guilt is 30 points
- Fear is 100 points
- Anger is 125 points

The dynamics of the ego are very strong in these lower emotions making one susceptible to low self-esteem and physical illness. Hawkins states that "excessive guilt and remorse are disguised forms of egotism in which the self becomes blown up, exaggerated, and the hero of the tragedy, the negativity of which feeds the ego" (p. 51). This is totally aligned with *A Course in Miracles* which states that guilt is not only not of God, but an attack on God. The error is inflated instead of being relinquished to a higher power. At one point Hawkins makes this strong statement: "Many people actually chose to die rather than face the inner conflicts and own the responsibility for either the conflict itself or for seeking help and resolution." The problem is that death is no solution. There is no escape from the consciousness level of yourself! You have to transcend these lower levels of emotions in order to get recalibrated at a higher level, which is the whole point of enlightenment and the whole point of life!

Hawkins has obviously studied *A Course in Miracles* carefully as his solution is: "By invitation of the Holy Spirit, it [one's life] will be transformed by the healing power of Grace." During a Liberation Breathing® session we invite and pull in the Holy Spirit, as nothing is too hard for the Holy Spirit to release.

Anger and Its Consequences

In this work, we study the consequences of anger, since we see so many relationships crash and so many bodies destroyed because of it. *A Course in Miracles* states that anger is never justified. And Jesus (the voice of *A Course in Miracles*) means *never*—not just sometimes. People will say, "I am not angry, I am just irritated." And yet the *Course* says irritation is just the tip of the iceberg covering up hate. In seminars, we list all the gradations of anger on the board:

- Irritation
- Being snippy
- Being snappy
- Sarcasm
- Put-downs
- Sneering
- Name calling
- Heavy energy
- Aggressiveness
- Defensiveness
- Bitterness
- Resentment
- Grudges

- Contempt
- Meanness
- Revenge
- Verbal abuse
- Anger
- Hate
- Rage
- Physical abuse
- Violence

It *all* has to be given up according to *A Course in Miracles* if you want to be enlightened. You will just keep reincarnating over and over until you give it all up. An angry person strives for power and domination (emphasized because it is a false power). Ammachi says that anger makes you weak in every cell of your body. The person really has an inferiority complex. They are intolerant of equals or superiors and must think they are superior to be happy. Anger is simply an expression of insecurity, inferiority, and false pride. *A Course in Miracles* says flat out that it is all just a cover up for fear. Angry people are those who are the most afraid. Dr. Hawkins says it is the ego's substitute for courage.

The consequences of anger are serious. Ill health will be the inevitable consequence. As a former nurse I can tell you there are circulatory changes; the heartbeat becomes rapid; the smaller blood vessels contract and go into spasm. You end up with higher blood pressure, the heart being overworked and circulation interfered with. The entire organism is disorientated. Digestion becomes disordered and the effectiveness of the immune system goes down. The more often you get angry the more you train the neural pathways of the brain, which leads to a downward spiral. Regularly getting angry makes you get even angrier.

The spiritual consequences are equally bad. Anger prevents you from reaching a higher level of consciousness, as Dr. Hawkins explains. Vibration occurs at a very low plane. The worst part as I see it is that it shuts out the mind of God! Furthermore, through anger and non-forgiveness much of the power gained by spiritual work on yourself can be lost. Your spiritual power is drained through every pore of your body when you get angry, as Ammachi said.

Anger produces fear and shutdown in relationships. Some of the most difficult cases we have ever worked with were people who had a birth script that led them to be angry (at the doctor for using anesthesia, forceps, or induction procedures, etc.). They were very angry at birth and they survived, so their particular script turned out to be, "I need anger in order to survive." It was very hard for them to give up anger because the way they had it set up was that if they gave up anger they would die. This kind of complex wiring from birth can be very hard on relationships. Fortunately, we know how to erase birth trauma and negative personal lies. It is so much easier to correct them than to stuff them, suppress them, wrestle with them, or pretend they are not there.

The Forgiveness Test

In my seminars, I always give everyone the "Forgiveness Test." On a sheet of paper draw a scale from 0 to 10 on which zero equals no forgiveness and 10 equals total forgiveness. On the scale, select the number reflecting the level of forgiveness you feel for key people in your life:
- mother
- father
- sibling(s)
- spouse
- ex(s)
- self

What are your scores? People score their levels of forgiveness astonishingly low. I try to move everyone to a 10, but it is a lot of hard work. If you are not at 10 on all persons, you are still angry. Then, I repeat the consequences of anger again, and still some hold out. Dr. Hawkins says that "Reluctance to forgive is a consequence not only of unwillingness to let go of the *ego juice* of perceived injustices, but also the illusion that others do not deserve forgiveness."

A Course in Miracles has some very strong statements on the topic of anger. It says, "You will attack (get angry at) what does not satisfy you to avoid seeing that you created it." Anger is a huge cop out! The *Course* also says, "Beware of the temptation to be perceive yourself as unfairly treated." That one is important because a lot of people use the excuse of how they were treated as a justification for their anger. And, yet, the *Course* repeatedly says, "Everything that happened to me I called for it." What is meant is you attracted it. If someone abused you, you attracted that with your suppressed negative thoughts and/or karma. The *Course* also says, "Defenses attract attack." In other words, if you use anger as a defense, you will simply get more attack coming at you.

It all becomes about your decision to cling to anger and get the "sick ego juice" as Dr. Hawkins calls it, or turn it over to the Holy Spirit and give it up. The consequences of that decision affect your brain chemistry. You may be angry that you are not getting a mate, not getting ahead, not feeling well, or that your life sucks. I assure you all these things are a *result* of the fact that you never gave up your anger in the first place. Your anger screws up your life, and then you get angry that your life is screwed up. It *won't work*. In Liberation Breathing® anger is pumped out gently on the exhale.

Babaji taught me the highest solution about anger. He said:
- You don't suppress it; that hurts your body.
- You don't dump it; that hurts others.
- You change the thought that causes the anger and you breathe out the charge.

This is the most effective way to handle anger I have ever heard of and that goes for all heavy emotions. They are spearheaded by thoughts. In regards to guilt, you have to state to your practitioner what you are guilty about, breathe it out, and then figure out what you are going to do about it. Karma means accountability. Every individual is answerable to the universe all the time. To clear your karma you can do good works, prayer, benevolent acts, and selfless service, which Babaji calls Karma Yoga.

A Tribute to Forgiveness—Markus' Birth Story

In one intense wet breathing session in a hot tub, I remember experiencing the intense fear, anger and resentment I formed around my birth of being induced! Because I was induced to come out I formed a huge authority case, distrust of so-called experts, and even a sense of anger and sadness that my mother did not stand up for my right to come out on my own. I discovered later why I did not want to come out in the first place. I perceived myself as a financial burden, which in fact I became after birth. My father lost his work due to illness and my family all moved back from California to Ohio, to live with my maternal grandparents for a spell. It was from Hollywood, where I was born, back to the hinterlands of small-town, rural Midwest. A bit of a come down at the time, but nevertheless the destiny I chose.

After I cleared my birth trauma of being induced, Sondra suggested we all do a "forgiveness diet" on both of our parents, the delivery team, our siblings and ourselves! Writing 70 times a day for seven days, "I forgive my mother completely," helped me to clear the unresolved anger I held at her from my birth. I did the same on my dad, my sister, the delivery team, and myself. I did another forgiveness diet on my former wife. It is very liberating to really let yourself off the hook, along with those from your past toward whom you have grievances. In fact, to be enlightened you cannot hold any grievances *at all*. *A Course in Miracles* teaches that until you forgive everyone one hundred percent you have not really forgiven at all…and as long as you hold grievances you will not know the power of unconditional love.

Part 7

Birth and Relationships

The Biggies—Negative Consciousness Factors

I met Leonard Orr in the 1970s. My friends drove me to where he was teaching to a group of about twenty on a hillside outside of Santa Cruz. On a flip chart he wrote what he called the "five biggies"—the five most negative consciousness factors that keep us from bliss:
- Birth trauma
- Specific negative thought structures
- The parental disapproval syndrome
- The unconscious death urge
- Other lifetimes

I looked at the list, knowing I had not handled any of the *that*. I figured somewhere on the list was the cause of my problems so I decided to surrender to him as a teacher. I walked up and asked him for a consultation.

I soon learned that Leonard had discovered what he called *rebirthing* by staying in a steam bath too long. He was found on the floor rolled in the fetal position regressed to early infancy. When he came back to present time, he found it amazing that he could remember that far back. Over a period of years, he experimented in home steam baths, staying in long periods of time which produced earlier and earlier memories. He eventually had a spontaneous memory of his birth, which for him was shocking and scary (because he had the umbilical cord wrapped around his neck multiple times at birth). When he finally healed his birth trauma, everything changed and became bright. He felt orgasmic. He knew that he had really discovered something and he sought to plan out a group experiment. I was lucky enough to be part of this first group.

Over time, Leonard added more categories, all of which can be cleansed from the body through conscious, connected breathing:
- *Birth Trauma* — all of the memories of our birth stored in our bodies
- *Specific Negative Thought Structures* — the negative thoughts about life, people, and ourselves accumulated since conception

- *The Parental Disapproval Syndrome* — the disapproval our grandparents gave to our parents, how our parents suppressed it and carried their disapproval down to us, and how we risk carrying it down to our children
- *The Unconscious Death Urge* — programming and decisions made about death and dying; the attraction to death.
- *Other Lifetimes* — past-life memories that affect us in this life
- *Church dogma* — guilt, separation, and negative beliefs instilled about our Creator and our relationship with Universal life force
- *School trauma* — conditioning about our country, society, and ourselves formulated through institutions and conventional education, including traumatic events that shaped our personalities
- *Senility* — which can be processed out before it is too late to turn it around. Leonard has written extensively on this subject. I have gone through it myself and have written about it in my book *Healing and Holiness*.

It is important to process all of these if you want to be liberated. In the Loving Relationships Training®, we cover these eight issues extensively and how they affect relationships.

Relationship Patterns

My particular research focus is in the area of how one's birth trauma affects one's relationships, life, and body. It is a fascinating topic, and I find people to be interested in this topic in every country in which I have worked. Most people wonder why, when they love each other so much, their relationships soon get stuck and become difficult or even impossible. I am excited to share the research I authored (first published in *Birth and Relationships*) about how birth types affect relationships. I suggest you read it all, including birth types other than your own. You may be living with someone who had a different type of birth, or you may have a boss, co-worker, friend, or child with a different birth type. It will give you a much deeper level of compassion and understanding of their behavior.

When clients continue with breathing sessions, their whole life becomes an open book for them to examine and purify. Besides birth material coming up, it is inevitable that issues related to relationships will arise. This is exactly why I wrote the Loving Relationships Training®. It is no mistake that it came through me very soon after Leonard Orr channeled rebirthing. Competent practitioners should not only take the LRT®, but it behooves them to review it so they can become experienced advisors on the topic of relationships.

In the Loving Relationships Training® we cover the 12 common relationship patterns:

1. Attracting a partner like your mother/father/caretaker
2. Recreating the way your parents treated you
3. Copying your parents' relationship with each other
4. The parental disapproval syndrome
5. Sibling rivalry and jealousy
6. The revenge pattern
7. The incest pattern
8. The helplessness pattern
9. The struggle pattern
10. The guilt pattern
11. Channeling the family mind
12. The sabotage pattern

We see these patterns come up in breathing sessions with clients all the time. Every LB® practitioner must recognize, understand, and be able to process clients on these patterns. In the LRT® we cover them in depth. Below, I discuss one of the most insidious, suppressed, and taboo patterns—the incest pattern.

The Incest Pattern in Relationships

Suppressed incest often stands in the way of physical affection. The point at which you could not receive physical affection from your parents (or they from you) is usually the point at which your sexuality became inhibited. This pattern may be experienced as:
- acted out incest in a family (from a parent, step-parent, cousin, neighbor, member of the clergy, etc.)
- emotional incest (which most of us have at varying degrees)
- suppressed incestuous feelings that come out obliquely

Infants naturally desire touch. The desire for more affection from our parents than we got inspires us to unconsciously set up our mates as our parents. The trouble is, the more we set up our partner as a parent the less we are able to make love to them because of the incest taboo. This does not usually come up early in a sexual relationship. It comes up later when the intimacy of moving in together or getting married is very strong and there are more memories of one's childhood household coming up. People often tell us that sex was great until the day that they got married! Below are examples of the incest pattern at various stages:
- If parents (during diaper changing, for example) are afraid of intimacy, the child senses it and interprets it as rejection.
- A young girl may enjoy sitting on her father's lap. One day he may suddenly get an erection and throw her off his lap. She is crushed and does not understand what she did wrong.
- A young boy who is used to being bathed and touched by his mother is suddenly told she cannot do that anymore and no explanation is given. Later this "shut-down" memory gets in the way of every touch. Touch becomes inhibited.
- A child makes the decision that since he cannot get physical affection from the one he really loves (the parent), then he is a failure and can't make it with those he loves. Thus, he can only have great sex with the ones he does not love as much (or a prostitute who is not the Madonna).

- A woman competes for men in an attempt to get "dad" away from "mom" by going for married men or men who are taken.

Triangles are a symptom of incest. When there is acted out incest, the one who received it may feel special and the ones who did not may feel left out. There is tremendous shame to be worked out in all cases. In the case of emotional incest, there is usually an extreme lack of boundaries. Examples include:
- a parent confiding sexual experiences with a child
- a parent walking around in the nude, over-stimulating a child
- a parent acting overly aware of a child's budding sexuality by making comments or inappropriate sexual remarks, or violating privacy
- a parent using a child to satisfy needs that should be satisfied by other adults
- a parent suppressing so much that emotional distance results

It is shocking how much sexual abuse we see in this work. The result is very complicated wiring in a client. The LB® practitioner must be very skilled to process it. On one hand, the practitioner needs tremendous compassion. On the other, practitioners cannot forget that *A Course in Miracles* teaches there are no victims. When a client accepts this, they quickly shift from blame into healing. The practitioner must teach forgiveness on all sides—forgiving the perpetrator and forgiving oneself.

We hear thousands of stories about incest and abuse. Fortunately, the breathing sessions are so powerful that these traumatic memories can actually be breathed out of the cells so they no longer run us or recreate similar situations as adults. If they are not released from the mind and body their imprint may lead to attracting abuse later in life, over and over.

Relationships in general improve a great deal after taking the LRT® and doing Liberation Breathing®. When you forgive completely, everything changes and improves. As you work out ego and conflict, you achieve more peace in all of your relationships. A person soon finds out that he or she wants to hang out with other people who are doing this kind of work and who share the same paradigm. At this point, it is good to practice the principle of right association. Higher people who are clear force you to adapt upward.

The Birth Script in Relationships

In the Loving Relationships Training® we teach an important lesson: "Love brings up anything unlike itself for the purpose of healing and release." When someone loves you, the energy of that love penetrates you and pushes out of you (like a master cleanser) whatever is suppressed: fear, guilt, anger, and negative thoughts. *Your* love is doing the same thing to your mate. While this *stuff* is coming out, the relationship can be strained and strange. The Loving Relationships Training® is designed to help you learn how to deal with these side effects. Liberation Breathing® helps you clear all of this.

The thoughts you had at birth—your *birth script*—will be pushed up and out of you. Examples of common thoughts and impressions derived at birth are:

- Life is a struggle.
- The universe is a hostile place.
- The universe is against me.
- I can't get what I need.
- Life is painful.
- Love is dangerous.
- I can't get enough love.
- People hurt me. Men/women hurt me.
- I can't trust men/women.
- I have to be angry in order to survive.
- I can't get out. (of the womb or the relationship which becomes a womb)
- I have to get out of here.
- I am not wanted.
- There must be something wrong with me.

Thoughts like these, plus your personal lie based on your particular birth trauma, will begin to surface. If you don't know about this and how it works, your relationships can get very crazy. Remember, these subconscious thoughts create results continually, which are often projected onto the partner. If a woman has the thought "men hurt me" (perhaps because she was hit on the butt by a male obstetrician), she will then be putting out that thought psychically in the form of a command like this: "Men, hurt me!" She will psychically demand this from her man or men, setting them up to hurt her to prove herself right. This is because love takes upon itself your negatives so you can see them more clearly. A mate will literally act out the negative thoughts of a partner in order to heal him or her, usually without realizing it.

What is really going on in most relationships is that *birth traumas are colliding*. Family patterns are dovetailing. Personal lies are clashing. One person's subconscious material is banging against the other person's subconscious material. With all of this going on, it is no wonder we have such a high divorce rate. I think it is really hard to manage a relationship when you do not know anything about your partner's birth script or his or her personal lies.

Another thing that comes up in relationships related to birth is "no-exit terror" manifested as "I have to get out of here." When intimacy is high and the love is intense, the energy usually stimulates memories of being crowded in the womb and being trapped. The feeling is then projected onto the relationship. Actual fear of suffocation could come up and cause a partner to leave suddenly for no apparent reason.

There may even be fear of pleasure in the relationship. That is because the bliss of the womb was followed by something painful and fearful (getting hurt in the birth process). A baby usually gets the thought "pleasure is followed by pain." Therefore, when the relationship gets too pleasurable, a tremendous fear can follow, causing a person to withdraw, leave, or stop the pleasure because they are afraid that pain will follow.

There is often a basic fear of letting go with another person, or even fear of touching that may not come up early in the courting period. After the couple begins to live together and when family and birth memories are activated, a person may start feeling unsafe about letting go or being touched because at birth that person was mishandled and became afraid. The more love a person feels, the more fear might come up because love's powerful energy triggers the memories.

In the beginning of a relationship most of these birth memories are suppressed. An example is extreme separation anxiety. A partner might be terrified of being left by a mate, or even being left alone. This again may not have been noticed in the courtship. We can often trace these fears back to the moment the newborn infant was suddenly taken away from the mother to a nursery where it felt abandoned. I have had clients cry for hours when re-experiencing that moment of separation from the mother.

There could be sex-identity problems related to birth that will affect a relationship. Perhaps the parents wanted a boy and got a girl. This girl may grow up feeling she is never good enough as a woman and may end up always feeling inferior to her husband. He may get tired of this low self-esteem and want her to leave. Fear of sex may show up (since sex leads to pregnancy and pregnancy led to birth, sex may *activate* subconscious memories of one's birth trauma). All of this could be just too much to deal with, so the easy way out could be to make sure that sex cannot happen.

Lack of breastfeeding can also affect a relationship. Some of these babies grow up feeling undernourished and never feel satisfied no matter what their mates do because their basic thought is "I can't get enough." Babies fed on demand may have a thought, "I can get anything I want whenever I want it." Babies fed on schedule may form a thought "I can never get what I want when I want it. I always have to wait." What goes on in the womb definitely affects relationships. I refer you to the brilliant research of Dr. Thomas Verny, who wrote *The Secret Life of the Unborn Child*.

Be patient and loving with yourself while you examine how your birth script is affecting your relationships. There is time. Pieces of your birth material may come up for years. You will let it up a little at a time, which will be safe for you. If you have a partner who is open to self-inquiry and is willing to purify his or her mind, then you are very fortunate indeed. Clearing all this can be a healthy and fun part of your relationship.

Case Study 1: "I began to tingle and hum in my hands and face. A pungent, yet not unpleasant, metallic taste appeared in my mouth, nose and throat. I had the image of being carried along gently yet powerfully on a river. My now more rapid breaths were the waves and troughs over which I plummeted, inexorably carried downstream toward a destination I could not see. I have the sudden realization that I am no longer in control. I am approaching the rapids. I am nearing the falls and there is not a thing I can do. My breathing has reached high gear. I am a fish thrown high and dry. Taking the plunge. Confusion! Bewilderment! I arch up in one final spasm! Then suddenly it is over. I am over too. Over the gap. Over the chasm. Over the abyss. Over the bridge! I made the whole distance but without a parachute, and I am smiling. In one moment out of time I am transformed from a chugging locomotive. Thirty-two years of hauling heavily laden freight cars up a never ending incline. Now I am free. Free, and free forever. I am free. My mind is reeling. I don't remember anything. I notice almost casually that I am in bliss.

"During my second rebirthing, I remembered being separated from my mother's body and being taken away to the nursery screaming and howling. I had emerged strong, healthy, breathing, and huge. I heard the doctor's voice as I watched myself being carried away to the nursery. He said, 'He's in fine shape now, he can take care of himself!' Those were his exact words. At the moment I most needed to be in the warm, safe presence of my mother, I was snatched away and placed all alone in the nursery! Those words, 'He can take care of himself' had become my reality. My song. My motto. My conclusion. I remembered making the decision on a feeling level: 'Okay, this is it. It looks like I'm going to have to do it all by myself.' Suddenly the whole story of my life unfolded as I saw how this decision had had an overwhelming and primary influence on my behavior. The revelation of this truth dredged up a bitter sadness over the loneliness I had endured as a result of this self-imposed, fierce self-sufficiency and independence. I saw clearly the struggle my life had been because I decided at birth never to share my burdens, tasks, endeavors or projects with others. More tears. Then I quietly resolved to let go of this decision and free myself of it. Gradually the slight paralysis left my extremities and melted away and was replaced by a pervasive glowing feeling of well-being and calmness. My environment and body became light and vibrant, like a slackened guitar string strummed again and again."

Affirmations that address many of the common themes related to birth trauma:
- I am breathing fully and freely.
- I survived my birth. My parents, my doctor, and I love life and I choose the divine plan of my life.
- My physical body is a pleasant and wonderful vehicle for my full and free self-expression.
- I am glad to be out of the womb so I can express myself fully and freely.
- I now receive assistance and cooperation from people necessary for me to carry out my highest good.
- I am safe and protected by Infinite Intelligence and Infinite Love. People and things no longer hurt me without my conscious permission.
- I am no longer afraid of my breath.
- I am now willing to see my birth clearly.
- Feeling all my emptiness won't destroy me.
- I forgive myself for the pain I caused myself at my birth.
- I forgive myself for the pain I caused my mother at my birth.
- Energy and vitality are my birthright.
- My mother loves and appreciates me.
- My mother is now glad that I was born.
- My mother is now happy to get me out of the womb.
- It was a privilege for my mother to have me, and an honor to bring me into the world.
- I am glad to be here. The entire universe is glad that I am here.
- I no longer feel unwanted. The universe rejoices at my presence in it.
- My mother, father, family, and friends are all glad that I was born and that I am alive.
- Praise the Lord for the perfection of my living spirit, mind, and body.

Conception Trauma and Affirmations

It is said that we are conceived in the image of God. Our conception in coming into this dimension, however, may feel less than Divine. There may be a *conception trauma*. Now it may really stretch your mind to find out that you can remember your conception. It certainly stretched mine, but one day I did! The research we have speaks for itself. We have had far too many cases where clients with traumatic conceptions re-created the circumstances of their origin in the conception of their relationships or the conception of businesses and projects. Examples include:

- A man conceived on his parents' honeymoon (after which they stopped having sex) married four times only to have each marriage take a sudden nose-dive during the honeymoon.
- A woman conceived in rape grows up to be the victim of sexual abuse.
- A client whose father died in war shortly after conception attracts a lover who dies shortly after the relationship begins.
- A client who was conceived the day the stock market crashed (when his father lost everything) has a pattern of creating a relationship, then going broke.
- A client conceived while his mother was a prostitute blames himself and feels he is bad. He falls in love with prostitutes and then is unable to make love to them because they reminded him of his mother. Like Oedipus, he is unconsciously drawn to the circumstances of his origin that manifested as an incest pattern.
- Unplanned conceptions can lead to unplanned relationships.
- Illegitimate conceptions can lead to sneaky relationships.

The circumstances surrounding your conception become the foundation of many unconscious patterns of memory in your life. One of my clients was conceived on a boat. Her most wonderful times were on her boat where she would float out to sea and play opera music and go into bliss (a good conception). Every relationship goes through a life cycle that reflects the dovetailing patterns of the participants—

conception, prenatal, natal, postnatal, infancy, childhood and adolescence. The stages of growth are recapitulated in the growth of every loving relationship.

If your origin is somehow unknown to you—stuck at some twist in your conception—then all your relationships could be misconceived. If your thought at conception was negative, then the conception of each of your relationships could be secretly doomed from the start! Your thoughts, after all, create your results. Below are examples of negative conception thoughts.

- I am not wanted.
- I am separate from God.
- I don't belong.
- I am a mistake.
- I don't want to be here.
- I cause separation. (a common thought resulting from coming between mom and dad, which can lead to incestuous triangles later in life)

Forgiveness is always the key. The affirmations below are designed to help heal conception trauma, and will vary according to one's particular circumstances:

- I chose to be here.
- I belong where I am.
- I am part of God's plan.
- My love is a unifying force.
- My body is a safe and pleasurable place to be.
- God is with me here and now.
- I am chosen.
- I have a purpose.
- I am excited about being here.
- All my choices are divinely inspired.
- I conceived of a great life and the best is yet to come.
- I forgive my parents for all their fears of having me.
- Thank God my parents had me.
- God wants me to be here.

Prenatal Trauma and Affirmations

The time the unborn child spends in the womb is, as Dr. Verny teaches, the busiest and the laziest days of our lives. We relax in a sea of supportive fluid, all our needs provided by our umbilical connection to Mother. We are in the ultimate support system available to man. Mission Control does all the work. We are in Eden. In later life we often seem to recreate the bliss of the womb—in bed with the covers pulled up, in the bathtub, in the hot tub, swimming, sailing, listening to music, watching a movie, or driving a car.

In relationships we often project the desire for the womb onto our partners, expecting them to provide that sense of infinite wellbeing we enjoyed in Mother's belly. This *umbilical attachment* results in inevitable separation, as the cord has to be cut at birth. To the extent that you feel you need your partner in order to survive, you may subconsciously push him or her away, proving to yourself that you are self-sufficient after all. When love is based on need, you always have a love/hate relationship. Werner Erhard said, "The only reason you need someone is to have them to blame."

The compulsion to create womb-like relationships leads to what *A Course in Miracles* calls the "tyranny of special relationships," where you place your partner on a pedestal above your fellow men and women. We once saw a greeting card which expressed this kind of relationship best. On the front cover it said, "It's you and me babe against the world!" Inside it said, "When do we attack?"

The womb is a busy time when the unborn child is growing rapidly—mentally and physically. The child is receiving information through its mother's neurological system as well as telepathically interpreting her feelings and reacting to their meaning. If you were unplanned, unwanted, an accident, illegitimate, or the "wrong sex," your nine months of hiding might have seemed like years of solitude, knowing that you were doomed to be a disappointment to those you loved.

If anything unusually good or bad happened in your family—or indeed in the world—while you were preparing yourself for this life, you probably absorbed the information on some level. If your mother sang to you, the song she sang may still be in your heart. You grew familiar with the sound of her voice, as well as her thoughts when she talked to or thought about you. In a very real sense, her thoughts were your thoughts, causing response in your highly sensitive little mind and body.

You took in a lot very quickly. Imagine being in hibernation for nine months on a spaceship, a mother computer feeding you data nonstop while your body grows and grows and grows. The container in which you rest seems to be shrinking as your body grows. Suddenly, a red neon sign lights up "NO-EXIT TERROR." You start looking for a way out, groping, creeping and crawling through the dark until you finally see a light at the end of the tunnel. When you come out of the womb, you fall head over heels into life. It's no wonder:

- we fear entrapment!
- we demand space in our relationships!
- commitment is such a confront!
- staying seems like a dead end!
- it seems like we have to leave to grow!
- we fear change, transition, the unknown, the future!

Affirmations for healing prenatal trauma:
- I am a child of God, nurtured in the universal womb of the Divine Mother.
- It is safe to stay.
- It is safe to leave.
- I am committed to my own wellbeing.
- All change leads me to my greater wellbeing.
- The unknown is safe.
- The future is full of wonderful surprises.
- When I let go I win.
- I am free inside.
- Since I am free, I no longer have to leave to feel free.
- I only depend on dependable people.
- It is safe to be close to people.

Infant Guilt and Affirmations

The Infant Guilt Syndrome describes the condition we take on at birth when we think our aliveness hurts our Mother, our source of life for nine months. We engage in our first experience of *separation*. As you squirm through the birth canal your mother's fear of re-experiencing her own birth is activated, causing her to hold on, shut down, and tense up, which in turn causes her fear and pain.

The "Infant Guilt" begins when you mistakenly conclude it is your presence that causes pain. "I always hurt the one I love," or "I am bad," may become a constant theme of your life. And so you separate from your own inherent goodness, as well as from God, as psychological and spiritual guilt join forces to make you feel alone in a cold, cruel universe.

You grow up with the fear of being seen, for example, as bad, causing you to hide in your relationships. You do not want others to notice how "bad" you really are, so you disguise yourself as a good girl or nice guy, seducing others into believing you are who you think you *are not*. Then you live in a constant fear of being found out, discovered for who you are, an imposter who really does not deserve love and happiness. *How could you?* You hurt people!

In your most intimate relationships, the delicate balance of your identity is severely threatened. The light of your partner's love will seek to shine on every shadow of your being. You will have a hard time hiding. You might try to shut down your joy and aliveness completely in a subconscious effort to protect your lover from the pain you anticipate causing. You want to hide your badness. Eventually you will explode, blaming your partner for your withholding pattern, and maybe even leave, thus completing the cycle of your birth scenario.

In most relationships, people tend to seek the lowest common denominator of aliveness, and then think their partner is boring or the relationship is dull. Boredom is the effort involved in suppressing something, and most people are walking cases of emotional anesthesia: suppressed joy and aliveness.

You may actually go so far as to leave your partner, claiming you have outgrown her or him, as if the relationship was a pot and you were the plant. This "outgrown myth" is another recapitulation of the prenatal entrapment and the no-exit terror you first felt at birth and have since held in your mind and body. No wonder an inordinate number of relationships end after nine months!

Liberation Breathing® supports you in locating and releasing this primal panic from your body so that you are no longer reacting to love with the mentality of a newborn. You can see which conclusions you made at birth no longer serve you.

Replace them with affirmations such as:
- I forgive myself for thinking I caused anyone pain.
- I am innocent.
- My aliveness is a pleasure to experience.
- My love is good enough for me and everyone else.
- I am good.
- My presence is a delight.
- I deserve to have it all.

Normal Birth

You may think it is not even necessary to mention a normal birth, believing that since there are no complications there is nothing to cover. That is exactly the problem. People who had normal births often feel like it was no big deal. Sometimes they feel like since it was nothing unusual, they are not as special as others who had more dramatic births. One client had the thought, "People don't like me for having it easy." He was always creating people judging him for having it easy.

Normal births can produce the following negative thoughts:
- I don't matter.
- I am nothing special.
- My life is just routine.
- People don't really notice me.
- I am just ordinary.
- I am boring.
- I am guilty for having it easy.

Case Study 1: A psychologist wrote us the following letter about the influence of his birth on his relationships. "The only thing my mother ever told me about my birth was that it was ordinary…average…normal. When I asked her if there was anything unusual, she'd say, "No, nothing. It was ordinary." All my life I have felt just ordinary. The truth is, I've had an extraordinary life: I was the best student in school, an excellent athlete, I am unusually successful in my work, and I've had a marvelous marriage for twenty-five years. But, whenever anyone asks me how I am doing, more likely than not I'd respond, "Okay, okay…about average." And that is how I've always seen myself and my relationships, nothing special. Just normal. I tend to assume that I am like everyone else, that everyone else thinks the way I do and I am surprised to find out people are different than I am. Also, since I suspect my birth was somewhat painful, I tend to feel that pain is normal, suffering is ordinary, and that since I must have hurt my mother at birth, I owe it to all women to make up for that original sin. Other than that, I never make waves."

It is important to know that in so-called normal births there is still plenty of birth trauma that needs to be worked out. The transition from a liquid environment to an atmospheric environment is a big shock. The cord is still often cut too soon. This produces fear, panic, choking, and the belief that the baby has to be turned upside down and spanked on the bottom to get it to breathe (since it was coughing and choking). Turning the baby upside down and spanking may seem to have been standard practice. However, this is extremely traumatic to a new born and, as we have now learned, unnecessary! This normally delivered baby is hanging there terrified it will be dropped, its spine suddenly straightened abruptly after having been curled up in the fetal position for all those months. Sudden change often results in back problems that are chronic and many other things chiropractors observe. Thankfully, this practice is being eliminated, but many adults were born when this was the common practice of a so-called normal birth.

One of the worst effects of a normal birth is getting hit or spanked to make one breathe. This results in immediately associating pain and fear with breathing, which further results in the habit of breathing shallowly on the inhale. This is one of the main, original purposes of rebirthing: to heal the damage done to the breath mechanism at birth. Most people are taking in very little air on the inhale, and forcing the exhale. Because we are sub-ventilating, the cells do not get the oxygen they need and deserve. This, in fact, is one of our theories about the cause of aging: the cells do not get enough oxygen and, therefore, whither and ultimately die.

In this work, we have seen people with very negative thoughts about breathing itself. This not only makes their sessions difficult, it makes their whole life difficult. Here are some of the negative memories that form in relation to breathing due to birth trauma:

- It hurts if I breathe.
- Breathing is followed by pain.
- I can't breathe.
- I am going to hold my breath to get even.
- If I breathe I will die.

Some of these thoughts eventually lead to respiratory disorders such as asthma, bronchitis, and emphysema. When we have clients with these conditions, we help them track down the connection to birth thoughts upon learning to breathe. Although these thoughts may have been suppressed for some time, resulting in no illness, when something came along to trigger the birth trauma, the person often flipped into an asthma attack. For example, a person who was a forceps birth may be fine until one day when he walks down a street and sees a crane used to build a high-rise. The crane subliminally reminds him of forceps, and suddenly he gets a migraine headache in his temples and doesn't know why. All circuits are triggered, and this leads to an asthma attack. It is not far-fetched. We have seen it often.

Other aspects of birth trauma in a normal birth may include the sudden temperature drop (approximately 30 degrees) from the warm womb to a delivery room that was very cold, bright lights that hurt the baby's eyes, abrasive rubbing of the newborn's tender skin (resulting in the fear of being touched), cold scales, noise, scary instruments, masks, psychic contamination from negative thoughts of the delivery team and their birth traumas contaminating the space, the absence of the father and so on.

In a relationship, a person who was a normal birth could feel as if they do not count, do not matter, and were nothing special to their mate. They could set up their mate to be more important.

If a person who was a normal delivery was hit at birth, he could have any number of resulting negative thoughts which would affect his relationships. A female may have the thought, "Men hurt me." With that thought she may constantly (unconsciously) be setting up her mate to hurt her, then blame him and try to get back at her obstetrician by getting back at her mate, or men in general, as a substitute. If a person was handled roughly in a normal birth he or she might have a fear of being touched, and this could lead to the dwindling or nonexistence of affection in a relationship. Fortunately, there are now changes being made in the birth process.

Some clients had normal births in which the mother had a great deal of shame and embarrassment about being exposed. Commonly, those people draw conclusions that often result in problems in their sex lives.

In some normal births we have studied, the doctors and delivery team were in an incredible hurry. Perhaps they had other deliveries to do. Often their reasons were understandable. In these cases, clients had the thoughts: "People don't care about me," or "People don't have time for me." This later affected their relationships because they repeatedly set up their mates to seemingly not care. Often they would plead for affection just at the wrong time, i.e., just at the time the mate was really busy. Then they would say, "See, he doesn't care about me. He doesn't have time for me."

Affirmations for normal births include the following:
- I am a unique individual.
- I am an important part of God's plan.
- I make a difference.
- I have a valuable contribution to make.

- I am an extraordinary human being.
- Being with me is exciting.
- I am God's gift to the world, and the world is God's gift to me.

Unwanted, Unplanned, or Illegitimate Births

Many children are unwanted, unplanned, or illegitimate. In the final analysis, no child is truly unwanted totally because parents' results really reveal their true intention, i.e., what they get is what they subconsciously most desire. Still, a child may feel unwanted, as though he or she were the last thing on his parent's mind. An unwanted child will have a difficult time growing up and feeling wanted as a mate. He will tend to have a problem believing his own worthiness of love, often thinking he doesn't even deserve to be alive. And if someone does come along who wants him deeply, he will play his parents' role and reject the love that is being offered. Such is the power of the loyalties of the unconscious mind. An unplanned child may be addicted to lack of organization in his life. *Not planning* becomes a way of survival.

If you were an "accident," then all your relationships can seem like accidents—chance encounters that happen to you. If you were illegitimate, your whole life tends to go underground. In some cases, a mother is so embarrassed about an illegitimate conception that she attempts to hide her pregnancy. The child grows up thinking that he must hide to survive. Often what he will hide most is his own sexuality. Sometimes he will have a problem legitimizing his life in any deep sense. We know one such case where a man could not pay his taxes, because he was terrified that if he became legitimate, they'd find out he was illegitimate.

We know another case in which a woman wouldn't get married because marriage was legitimate and she wasn't! She was the illegitimate daughter of a famous politician, and she would never tell us who it was. As a baby, her mother would bring her to a prearranged street corner, where the father's black limo would be parked so he could see his child. This woman grew up to have very sneaky relations and strange rendezvous in bizarre places.

Case Study 1: "I knew I was unwanted. So I delayed coming out. I was late and very big, causing my mother pain. I felt rejected by both my parents. I never feel ready for a relationship, yet I crave closeness. I struggle like mad to avoid rejection, but I always feel there is something wrong with me. I want to be more intimate but rejection is always inevitable. I am always trying to prepare myself for the worst."

Case Study 2: "I was illegitimate. I wasn't supposed to be here. The way my birth affects my relationships is that I am very nervous about getting started in a relationship, and it causes a lot of upset for me. Thinking about relationships causes my stomach to be upset. I'd love to be in a relationship, but I have learned to function very well without one. I feel unworthy, unwanted, and unlovable."

Affirmations for unwanted, unplanned, and illegitimate births:
- I choose to be wanted.
- It is safe to be wanted.
- I am wanted as a man/woman.
- I deserve to be alive.
- I am irresistible.
- I am God's gift to the world, and the world is God's gift to me.
- I forgive my parents for not having the self-esteem to want me.
- I have the legitimate right to be loved and wanted.
- I am a chosen child of God.

Wrong Sex at Birth

In many Loving Relationships Training® seminars we do a survey in the birth section and ask, "How many of you were not born the sex your parents wanted?" You would be amazed at the number of hands that go up! Maybe both parents wanted a baby of the opposite sex from what they got, or maybe just one of the parents did. Either way, you can imagine how the baby feels! Remember always that the baby in uterus is a conscious, thinking being. It already knows if the

parents want the opposite sex from what it is. Many do not want to come out into that impending doom; they know they will be a disappointment. Some of the thoughts these babies have are:
- I'll never be good enough (as a woman or man).
- I am a disappointment.
- I am the wrong one.
- I am confused (in the case where one parent wanted a boy and the other a girl).
- I'll never be able to please people.
- I should be a boy (decision made by female baby if parents wanted a boy).
- I should be a girl (decision made by male baby if parents wanted a girl).

In most cases, the child feels hopelessness or doom until he or she gets clear on the perfection of his or her choice of gender in this life. In a relationship, the person feels he is never ever going to measure up. Let's say a female baby grows up in a family where they want a boy. She may become a tomboy in order to please the parents. If she does become feminine and creates a relationship with a man, she may pick one that will subtly or overtly put her down so she can feel not good enough as a woman. She could keep trying and keep failing. The problem is she will tend to pick a mate who will perpetuate the issue, a mate who probably has the *need* to put women down. This destructive game will go on and result in hurt until the partners see the truth and do something about it.

In my own case, my sister wanted a baby brother and my dad wanted a son. Later in life, I was too much in my masculine side and I was subtly competing with men in many ways that were not obvious to me…mainly intellectually. A woman in this case may also have trouble receiving from men. She may always be giving men a double message, "treat me as a woman, but I really require that you treat me as a man." A woman in this situation has to learn that she can please people by being a real woman.

In all cases of this type, we would ask the clients to take responsibility for the fact that they chose to incarnate into a family where the family wanted something other than who they were. We would ask them why they did not want to be wanted for the sex they were. When my first rebirther asked *me* that, I was stunned. I realized that I had agreed to come down as a leader in this life, but I had a lot of hesitancy doing it as a female. I was used to leading as a male in other incarnations. This was part of my conception trauma and getting clear on my own confusion upon incarnation got me out of the helpless victim mode. Although I could not change my sexuality, I could get clear that I wanted to be a woman, God wanted me to be a woman, and it was okay to be a woman now. I actually had to write this affirmation: "I forgive myself for being confused about being a female and not wanting to be wanted as a female due to this, and then blaming others."

Future parents should be, and often are, pleased with whatever sex they are given, and understand that it is perfect for them. It is ideal that this level of acceptance be reached *before* conception, and not just at birth or during the pregnancy.

Case Study 1: One of my clients was born to a wealthy man who gambled in Monte Carlo and bet a lot of money that he would have a boy. He had a girl. She grew up hearing from her father the often-repeated statement, "You cost me a lot of money because you were a girl." She adopted the thought, "I cause men to lose money!" In her life she married two millionaires. They both lost almost all their money when they were with her.

Case Study 2: "My parents wanted a boy, especially my father. This made me flip over and I was the opposite presentation of normal: face presentation. I was the opposite of what he wanted so I thought I had to always do the opposite of what people expected. I have always rebelled my whole life. One way was to choose to marry a man who was really the opposite of what my family and even myself wanted for me. My family was rich. He was definitely poor. In my past relationships I had been very argumentative. I would always take the opposite viewpoint from my mate. If he said the sky was blue, I would find a way to disagree about the sky no matter what. I could not be agreeable. My dad always took me to sporting events as if I was his little boy. I tried to do things that would make my father proud so I was very athletic. It was always easier for me to relate to male friends. But some of these friendships would lead to being lovers, and then sex would become a problem for me. I did not know how to act as a girl. Fortunately this all shifted through rebirthing as I learned how to enhance my feminine side. Sex finally improved, but, for a while, I was so confused I attracted gay men. I finally got through that also."

Affirmations for wrong-sex births:
- I am the right one.
- My sex is right for me.
- I am a wonderful surprise.
- I am God's gift to the world.
- I forgive myself and my parents for not knowing what we really wanted.
- I am desirable.
- I am irresistible.
- My body suits my Divine purpose.
- I am highly pleasing to myself in the presence of others.
- People are pleased by my presence.
- My presence is a complete pleasure.

Previous Miscarriages, Abortions, or Fetal Death

Whenever we interview a new client, we always find out if any miscarriages, abortions, or fetal deaths occurred prior to the pregnancy of that person. This is important information for several reasons. The mother was likely to be very worried about the possible death of this next being. This creates "prenatal trauma" and adds a lot of fear to the pregnancy and consciousness of the person who was in the womb. The person often ends up with fear of loss, fear of death, and generally feels unsafe in the world. If there is an abortion prior to this baby the mother may still be suffering from a lot of guilt, which will also affect the pregnancy and the baby. If a former baby died in uterus, or was a full-term fetal death, the new baby often feels he is supposed to be a replacement for the one who died. This creates added psychic pressure and ramifications.

Sometimes the former baby was actually the same soul, but did not make it the first time. I usually ask: "Does it seem like the baby that miscarried or died or was aborted before you might actually have been you?" Often times this question produces an immediate emotional reaction and the person feels with certainty that yes, it was actually so. In this case, this being may have the thought: "In order to live, I have to die first." These people tend to create what we would call a lot of *mini deaths* before they can enjoy life. They end up with the dilemma, "The more I live, the more I have to die." It is very complicated *wiring* in the mind, and it took us many years to learn how to unravel it.

A female client in Seattle related to me that her mother had seven male babies, all full-term fetal deaths before she herself was finally conceived. These pregnancies were all *her* trying to come in as a male, but because of her particular karma, she could not make it as a male and finally gave up. This is an extreme case.

Although we are careful not to add any guilt around the abortion issue, it is something that the practitioner and client must face if it is part of that person's case. If there was an attempted abortion that failed, the client sometimes goes through the whole memory. So we have to help them forgive everything. By helping them take responsibility for choosing their parents, they can get unstuck from the blame and anger. We would try to get back to why that person chose to be part of an abortion or attempted abortion. Some of these people grow up with the fear that someone is out to kill them.

Saddam Hussein was an extreme case in which his mother tried to abort him multiple times because Mohammed appeared to her telling her she was carrying an evil being. He survived, so she tried to kill herself by jumping off a bridge during the last trimester. She still survived and so she gave up. Look at how deranged he became. He took it all out on others.

Most often these people have the thought, "I shouldn't be here." Trying to live a life with that thought is definitely difficult and no fun! The liberation for

these people is, once again, getting out of blame and forgiving oneself for setting up that drama:
- I forgive myself for not wanting to live fully and for blaming others.
- I forgive myself for using others to end my life.
- Now I choose to be totally alive and live fully.

Case Study 1: An actor wrote us the following: "My mother had a miscarriage. Then she got pregnant with me. She was afraid she'd lose me too. I have always felt like I might be the wrong one—maybe that I wouldn't be here if the first child hadn't been miscarried. In my career as an actor, I find it hard to take parts away from other actors. I am guilty when I do get parts. I live in constant fear of getting replaced."

Case Study 2: A practitioner wrote us the following: "One of my clients had an interesting experience. His mother tried to abort him three times during the pregnancy. He grew up, fell in love and got married. Every three years he and his wife had a major upheaval. They even got divorced three times, every three years."

Affirmations for those born after previous miscarriages, abortions, or fetal deaths:
- The more I live the more alive I am. The more alive I am, the more I live.
- I can survive without being dead. I can survive being alive.
- Life is safe, living is safe. The more alive I am, the safer I am.
- I can start living right away and keep on living.
- I can let go of death and survive.
- I am safe and immortal right now.
- There is nothing to fear. I am alive. I am life itself.
- The more I give up worrying, the more alive I am.
- Life is what I want.
- I am responsible for my own joy and pain and others are responsible for their own joy and pain.
- People are happy that I am here.
- People always get better in my presence.

- People are glad that I am alive and they feel more alive in my presence.
- I forgive everyone and everything during my pregnancy and birth.
- The more I choose to be here, the better everything gets. And the better everything gets, the more I choose to be here.

Premature Birth

In the case of premature birth, we try to discover why this person came out of the womb early. There is usually some specific reason that he or she did not naturally stay in for the full time. Perhaps the mother was sick or the vibrations inside the mother were not good, and the person actually felt unsafe staying inside. There could have been what we call a *toxic womb*. Someone may have been worried about the baby's survival. These babies often develop thoughts like, "I am weak," "I am too small," "I am frail," or "I can't make it."

The incubator period for an infant born prematurely produces a considerable amount of trauma. When a baby is fed intravenously, there is a problem with small veins, so needles may be placed in the scalp or feet. In order to keep the needles from coming out, the baby is often tied down. When you imagine a newborn being tied down inside of a box, you can see why this baby usually ends up thinking: "I am helpless," or "I can't help it." This may become a life-long pattern.

Incubator babies often grow up with a psychic wall of some kind around them, which they think they need in order to survive. This wall could take the form of being *invisible*, yet difficult to penetrate. Or, it could take the form of being overweight, which is used for protection. The psychic wall represents the incubator. Very often a premature person has the thought "look but don't touch" so they unconsciously keep people away, especially affectionately and sexually. After all, family members have to peer through glass to see them! One of my premature clients was like this and attracted peeping toms. She came to me with that presenting complaint, without having made any connection to her birth until I pointed it out.

Once I had a client who kept having the following dream: She would see hands coming down through clouds over and over. These hands would be coming at her. Since I had been a nurse, it was easy for me to understand her presenting complaint. She was in an incubator after birth. She worked out a lot of her incubator trauma with me. In nursing school the way we bathed preemies was to put on gloves, put a bowl of warm water in the incubator and put the baby in the little bowl. (It was shocking to me how these little babies could fit in a little bowl.)

Usually a premature incubator person has to be rebirthed double. They not only have to be rebirthed out of the womb, but also out of the incubator. They may set up a room in their house as the incubator or their house as the incubator. They may set up their relationship as the incubator. The relationship then becomes a life/death situation to which the person clings desperately in an unhealthy way, even though they may think their health depended on it. If you encourage them to free themselves from it, it may appear to them you are nearly killing them.

Sometimes premature people are physically unhealthy. They may even look as though they are not fully born. By changing the thoughts "I am weak and helpless," they can make a lot of progress health-wise. We usually acknowledge them for having a strong enough life urge that they could survive incredible odds. Although their life urge was weak and created their barely making it, we try to reinforce and emphasize that part of their life urge that did pull them through was strong. It also helps to encourage them to go for spiritual nourishment. Body work is important as well.

These people must be encouraged to see that they can be independent and survive. The trouble is that they attract people who need someone dependent on them (which reinforces the incubator neurosis). Becoming very aware of these patterns is the first step, and consciously working on them in the breathing process has produced marvelous results.

Case Study 1: "I was premature—born at six and a half months. I was put in an incubator for seven weeks—my parents visited me every day and began willing me to live. My father was really afraid that I would not make it. The way my birth affects my relationships is that I seem to get only so close, and then create a glass wall. I never seem totally bonded with a man. I want to get married, but create men who don't want to…I have been very independent and want to prove that I can do it myself, and make it by myself. I love being the focus of attention but feel embarrassed when it happens. I seem to frighten lots of men, like I did my father and the obstetrician who was also scared I would not make it. I end up in look-but-don't-touch relationships."

Case Study 2: "I was two months premature and spent three months in an incubator. In my relationships I never feel touched enough. I feel a lot of anger about this. I want love but don't know how to receive it. I want to be touched and helped; but I didn't know how to accept it before breathwork."

Case Study 3: "I was in an incubator separated from my family for 2-3 weeks. I was not touched by my mother until I went home. I was premature by two months. So, the timing of my birth was a surprise and this created urgency and intensity and concern over life /death. My relationships always seem to be intense like that. I feel urgency as to where it is headed. They have to wait for me to be ready to love me and I have to stay separate from them when intense feelings come up. I notice that the time I always think is appropriate is somewhere between two and three weeks; then I can be with them again. Anytime sooner feels like the relationship will die. I generally create relationships with people who are not demonstrative about their feelings…they don't touch or hug."

Affirmations for premature births:
- I have everything I need to get everything I want.
- I am just the right size.
- I am enough, I have enough, I do enough.
- I am strong and safe.
- It is safe to be touched and I easily create that.
- I am healthy and alive all the time.
- All my arrivals and departures are easy.

- It is safe for me to come out and live outside the box.

Caesarian Birth

In one sense, caesarian births have it easier. They don't have to plow through the birth canal to make it; nor do they have to be as guilty about causing their mothers pain. The caesarian child, however, often suffers from interruption syndrome, since his original direction in life was rudely interrupted by the obstetrician. Nowadays there is a proliferation of caesarians often simply to please the doctor or fit his schedule. This kid will often grow into a headstrong adult who insists on doing things his own way, often at his own expense. At the same time, the more he insists on going his own way in life, the more likely he is to attract unforeseen interruptions blocking his path. He seems to want to make the journey through the birth canal he never made in the first place. He knows he knows how to do it, if only everyone else would leave him alone! But they never do. People get in the way. Often when caesarians have breathing sessions they will create constant interruptions to upset themselves, reliving the confusion they experienced when coming out. Practitioners should always ask if the caesarian was planned or emergency, as different conditions and thoughts emerge.

Relationships for a caesarian birth tend to be characterized by conflicts of will, changes of heart and mind, and constant disruptions. We know several caesarian couples and usually they are looking for someone outside the relationship to tell them what way to go in life, then resenting it and doing the opposite. If one partner is a caesarian and the other is not, the latter can be set up to be the obstetrician who should bail him out.

Support can be a major issue for caesarian. On the one hand, they want it desperately; on the other hand, they mistrust it and see all support as manipulation, interference, and opposition. "I want to do it my way" is the cry of the caesarian who at the same time is thinking, "I better get some help or I will never get out of this." This double bind produces confusion. Sometimes they create drama and have to wait for someone to *lift them out* of the mess. They do have the potential for seeing the easy way out at times. When they relax into this knowledge, they are a vast storehouse for shortcuts in life. Once they get over their guilt for not doing it the hard way in the first place, they can enjoy the innocence of their own intuitive know-how. Every birth contains an unknown gift.

I have had clients who were caesarian births with either terror or fascination with knives. Once I went to the home of a client and he had a knife collection on the wall. A female client told me she used to go hunting with her father and she became very good at skinning the animals. The worst-case scenario was a guy who was suppressing all his anger, partly at being a caesarian. One day his wife flipped out and with a knife started slashing the stuffed furniture! She was not at all the type to do something like that, but believe it or not, she was acting out his caesarian. (What you suppress, someone in your house might express.)

Case Study 1: "At my birth the doctors came into the womb with a knife to get me out. I felt like my space was invaded without my permission. Today I feel that sometimes people come up and want to get inside my space, and I don't want them there. I feel the same inability to effectively communicate to them to leave me alone. Since I was removed from my mother without her touching me, I felt very rejected…and I have always been afraid of rejection. I felt very angry and humiliated at my birth, because the doctors and nurses did not receive my communication. Since I did not get out of the womb by myself, I get afraid that emergencies are going to happen, and I need to be surrounded by people capable of saving me. I thought I hurt my mother at birth because of the incision and I am always thinking people are accusing me of causing them pain."

Case Study 2: "I was a transverse lay (sideways) caesarian with anesthetics and asleep three days after it all because of the anesthesia. I have great difficulty going directly towards people and careers that I really want. Even very big decisions are made very quickly—caesarian style. Once I arrive in a relationship, city, or career, it is often not clear how I got there. And I spend some time in the early stages somewhat unconscious."

Case Study 3: "During any relationship that I have, I immediately feel as if I am at the effect of the other person. I create men to be my obstetrician. Being smothered is a feeling I usually get when there is love present…so I feel I need to leave my body. I got a lot of anesthesia at birth so when I am touched my body feels numb with anesthesia. I never feel I can do anything myself, and when I do, my body goes numb, and it is as if I never accomplished anything. During my birth, I felt a knife come to my back but it did not touch me, so often I feel that support will kill me, and I am suspicious. During my birth, I believe I was going to decide to be born when I wanted to, but the doctor decided instead. So during sex when I feel I am about to climax, I feel that it will be taken away from me. Instead of being disappointed by my mate, I cut off myself first by going unconscious."

Affirmations for caesarian births:
- I am innocent.
- My way is the right way.
- I can always find the easy way.
- I'm right in the first place.
- All my interruptions are for my highest good.
- I forgive my mother and the obstetrician completely.
- It is safe to do things differently.
- I forgive myself for doing things differently.
- I deserve all the touching and holding I desire.
- I am always in the right place at the right time.
- I can trust my intuition.
- It is safe for me to complete things.

Induced Birth

Ordinarily a baby comes out when it is ready and begins the process of labor by emitting its own hormone. An induced birth is one in which the labor is artificially started, usually by intravenous drip. Sometimes there are medical reasons for induction. Sometimes there are less important reasons, even as ridiculous as the parents wanting to have the baby before New Year's eve to save on taxes or because the doctor has a golf tournament. Or perhaps someone wanted the baby to be born on an ancestor's birthday. Although it may seem innocent and logical at the time, if those involved knew the effect of this on the baby, we doubt seriously they would ever try for an induction.

People whose birth was induced often have trouble getting started. They may have to be *induced* into new things that they want or need to do. Although they may not be overtly angry, the anger of an induced person is often more suppressed and covert. They usually resent that their life started on other people's terms. They may actually get even in life for this by withholding. They may withhold love, withhold sex and affection, or withhold themselves from the world in general by withholding their power, their creativity, their mission, or contribution.

They may be putting out a vibration like this: "Come and get me. But if you do, I will resent it. I will say no to you to prove I can come on my own terms, on my own time." They often keep people waiting and wonder why people are upset about that. An induction type of person has not totally chosen to be here. Somebody else chose and they therefore may only half participate in life. In a relationship they may hold back until their mate finally starts pushing them or inducing them. Then they will resent it and say no. This will go around and around, over and over again as the birth script is run and rerun in frustration until one gets fed up. Sometimes if the recreated induction is gentle by the opposite mate, the situation produces good results. And these people become very productive once someone gets them started. However, because the induced person feels a need to say no in an attempt to get even, the opposite mate may not be so gentle. He or she may unconsciously become the obstetrician in the relationship even by getting pushy and panicked—"this baby has to be delivered *now*" scenarios. This makes the induced person balk, retreat, get angrier, and withhold more.

The severity of this repetitive game often depends on the reason that the induction was done in the first place. If the reason was to please the parents, the person may have a stronger desire to get even and the game is turned up! The attitude becomes, "I will do it on my terms, never on yours." We have met people that were actually induced to save a few hundred dollars on taxes. This, as you can imagine, often results in a tremendous charge around money. Some of these people work hard *not* to make money to get even.

Relating to someone who was induced requires a tremendous amount of patience. They tend, however, to attract partners who have little or no patience. This can be an unending battle unless both are very enlightened and are very willing to release the pattern and help each other. When it is happening, one could make light of it and say, "Now I am going to induce you." If said in the right voice it could work, especially if both are doing Liberation Breathing®.

Induced births tend to have problems with commitment—usually because their partners have to induce them into choosing the relationship. One can easily see how important this would be in a work situation. The employee may be a very, very good worker and just have trouble getting started or showing up on time. If the employer knew something about inductions, he could be more compassionate and not feel like he had to fire the person for just this reason.

Case Study 1: "I was induced because the doctor felt I was ready to be born. My mother was 37 at the time and had had a difficult time with my elder sister during her birth. I have always had problems with time. I am always late and pushing and feeling panicky. A major result of being induced is to want a man to do it for me, because I can't get started; but I resent him for pushing me. I do not believe I can choose a relationship."

Case Study 2: "I was induced because my sister, who is three years older than I, came out early. So I was induced to keep me from being early. (Does that make any sense?) My mother was drugged and my father was not there. I think I need to be drugged to have sex. I feel like men try to stop my growth or swallow my power (like my obstetrician did). People always have to induce me into a relationship and nobody ever wants me the way I am. I have a hard time starting projects."

Affirmations for induced births:
- It is safe to choose.
- It is safe to make up my own mind.
- I no longer need to create others inducing me.
- I'm in touch with what I desire.
- It is safe to express myself.
- It is safe to assert myself.
- I forgive myself for waiting, controlling, and blaming.
- I choose life.
- I control my own destiny.
- All my choices support my wellbeing.
- I can get started on my own.

Breech Birth

A breech baby comes out backwards, either buttocks first or feet first (which is more rare and known as *footling breech*). As practitioners, we study why this person turned around in the womb in the first place, since a baby intuitively knows the right way to be delivered. A breech usually turns because he or she was afraid or resistant to come out. Often he sensed some immense problem on the outside, some danger he saw that made him or her to want to go back! Or maybe he knew that one or both of his parents wanted a baby of the opposite sex and he wanted to avoid disappointment. Some babies actually think, "Oh no, not *this* family!"

Since this kind of birth is obviously harder on the mother, these people grow up with more guilt. They tend to have a fear of hurting people, especially women. In the Loving Relationships Training® they express thoughts such as, "I cause pain," "I have to hurt women (or people) to survive," and "I am guilty."

Arriving breech tends to make things harder in life. He or she tends to turn everything into more of a struggle than it need be. They might even do things backwards. One footling breech always put his shoes on the wrong feet, and as an adult he felt he always put his worst foot forward in relationships.

In some cases, the doctor may have attempted to turn this baby manually from the outside in order to get its head down. This is very painful to mother and baby; it definitely adds trauma. Sometimes a caesarian is required.

A breech needs to learn that he can have it easy and survive. A breech needs to learn that it is safe to come out. In a relationship, a breech may unconsciously hurt his partner and then feel terribly guilty, but will tend to re-run this pattern as long as he thinks his life depends on it. One of the very first cases we had at the beginning of rebirthing was a man who was quite suicidal. His presenting complaint was that he was constantly hurting others and could not stop. And he was so guilty about this he wanted to kill himself. At his birth, when he came out breech, his mother bled a lot and almost died. Therefore he was terrified to be inside a woman's vagina. Once he was able to connect his suicidal urge to his birth type (which he could not see before rebirthing) a great deal of it just lifted off during the breathing session. The progress he made in just one rebirthing session was astounding.

A breech case needs a lot of release from the thought that he needs to hurt others in order to survive. This addiction to hurting others (unconsciously of course), feeling guilty, punishing oneself for the guilt, then running the whole tape over and over again is a deep habit glued to the birth script. The problem is compounded because these birth types might tend to pick partners who have a masochistic desire to be hurt. This reinforces the pattern and the game. Both partners need to acknowledge their role in the game, and probably, both should do Liberation Breathing®, if not with the same practitioner, with two practitioners who can consult with each other.

We had several breeches whose personal lie was, "I am wrong." They are going the wrong way and always felt wrong, no matter how much we worked with them. Finally I realized that they had the thought that it was wrong to give up the thought, "I am wrong." After that, they finally made some progress.

Case Study 1: "I was breech. Labor was very long and painful for both me and my mother. The ambivalence about leaving the womb carries over to my relationships. I am ambivalent about being in a long-term relationship. I felt really lost upon being separated at birth from my mother. In relationships I tend to back out when there is too much closeness. Because the birth was long and painful, I blamed the male doctor for not fixing it."

Case Study 2: "I tend to think men are not really interested in or sensitive to women's feelings, especially pain. Men don't really care! Birth was a struggle. Life is a struggle, and relationships are a struggle. Pain follows pleasure, and has since birth. If I experience a lot of pleasure in a relationship, I'll often create an upset to follow."

Affirmations for breech births:
- I forgive myself for thinking I do it wrong.
- I forgive myself for the pain I think I caused others.
- My aliveness is safe and pleasurable for me and everyone else.
- It is safe to have life be easy and pleasurable.
- I am completely innocent.
- I can now get off to a good start.
- I can easily now go in the right direction.
- My way is the right way.
- I can take any turn I choose.
- It is safe to go my own way.
- I can survive without fighting and struggling.

Forceps Birth

Babies born with the help of forceps had their heads scrunched, screwed, twisted, and pulled out of the womb. Imagine being a tooth pulled out of your own mouth and you'll get the idea. *Why does a baby need forceps?* Because it is too big, too slow, too twisted, or too far down the canal for a caesarian section. Whatever the reason, it is stuck and the obstetrician sees his role as the liberator. Later in life forceps babies tend to create the same pattern of getting stuck, then attracting someone to bail them out at the last minute.

Forceps babies often develop migraine headaches as adults, and, even worse, life itself can become one huge headache for them. Sometimes during a breathing session, you can actually see the impression of the forceps on their temples. These might be feisty kids, spunky street fighters full of life and the desire to do things their own way. They don't usually trust support—*can you blame them*? In their minds, trusting equals having their heads handed to them! "No, thank you," is often their response to people who offer assistance. Support equals pain.

Since forceps are extremely painful to the soft-skulled baby, even the slightest remembrance of this experience is intolerable. Seeing a crane on the street or tongs in the kitchen could suddenly awaken the memory. Since the forceps birth type is often terrified of being manipulated by others, he will be obsessed with being in control, playing the obstetrician, turning the tables on the birth scenario, gaining the upper hand. The best thing to do with forceps people is to support them gently in following through on choices they make for themselves. Don't be too helpful, however, or they will think you are out to get them.

Once I gave a chiropractor in Puerto Rico a breathing session. He said he had waited years to get rebirthed because he felt he might die or lose his head in a rebirthing, and he felt I was the only one who could *handle* him. During the rebirthing he was sure his head was going to come right off! You can see why he chose that particular career.

Case Study 1: "Since my obstetrician was a stiff, authoritarian German, I don't like authority figures and have never gotten along with them. However, since I had to be helped along with forceps, I feel I need help in getting started with anything. Actually I have too much dependency and need, and resist help. I hate being manipulated or pushed in any way...I feel the world is dangerous. I have never felt responsible or that I could be responsible for my life."

Case Study 2: "My birth was somewhat difficult because I was a large baby. I was stuck in the canal—my shoulder was caught. So forceps were used. As a result, I get angry when others interfere in my relationships. I struggled a lot, and in the past I certainly acted that out in my relationships, especially the intimate ones.

Perhaps the main thought I have is that to be successful in relationships I have to leave. It is a lose/lose situation. Either my relationships have been filled with struggle and danger, or I leave them behind, thinking that to be a successful completion. Thank god all this is changing with breathwork."

Affirmations for forceps births:
- I forgive my obstetrician completely.
- I can do it on my own.
- I know how to make it.
- I always find endings easy and pleasurable.
- Since I can do it on my own, it is safe to let others help.
- I now experience all support as self-support.
- I can now see that people who want to support me want to bring me pleasure and make life easier.
- I no longer fight support.
- I am heading for more ease and support.
- My head leads the way to ease and pleasure.
- My heart safeguards my head no matter what.

Drugs at Birth

When a mother is drugged while giving birth, the drugs cross the placenta (which acts more like a sieve than a barrier), and the baby is drugged when born. And then we wonder why we have a drug problem in the world! People who were drugged at birth are often born lifeless and spend their whole life in a fog.

We were absolutely amazed to find that during breathing sessions, we could actually *smell* the drugs as they were breathed out. In one extreme case, Leonard and I were rebirthing a psychiatrist in Paris. During the second half hour of his breathing, not only could we smell the drugs, but we got very dizzy and nearly passed out. We spontaneously ran to the window and stuck our heads out to get fresh air! This man told us he had never had surgery or anesthesia after his birth (drugs from his birth were coming out of the cells). He shouted out after his session, "I have never felt this alive in my whole life!"

Clients who had a lot of anesthesia at birth often go *unconscious* during the breathing session. A well-trained LB® Practitioner knows a lot of ways to get them through this, although it may take a while. People who were heavily anesthetized at birth generally take longer in the process. These people may also go unconscious in their relationships and at work. They often have trouble getting up in the morning. Their medicine cabinet might be full of drugs, or they may get stoned a lot on marijuana or even become drug addicts. They may even recreate the need for surgery in their lives so they can relive the anesthesia experience. Subconsciously they think they need it, and can resolve it by working it out by reliving it.

On one occasion I facilitated a session for an experienced rebirther. Since he was a rebirther himself, he had the stamina and awareness needed to make a real study of his anesthesia case. He was able to get down to the exact thoughts he had had when the anesthesia took over his body. One minute he claimed to feel totally alive, ready to live fully and be born. The next minute, when the anesthesia crossed the placenta, he said, "Now I am turning to stone. My mother feels dead too…have I killed her? I cannot move. I am completely helpless." In his life he had had a problem with helplessness. He was very brilliant, but would periodically get helpless. We were able to make a lot of progress with that issue in the session. I felt great sadness myself during this session and cried when he recalled the anesthesia taking over his body. It seemed like he went from being totally alive to being dead right before my eyes! I recalled how he would often *haze over* and go into something I called *corpse consciousness*. Fortunately cold water rebirthing (an advanced technique that should not be tried alone) helped him a great deal, and he became a compassionate rebirther.

The worst case I had was a client with narcolepsy who had an overdose of anesthesia at his birth. He would fall asleep standing up in any place, at any time, and without warning. He had been through years of therapy to no avail. The trouble I had was I could not keep him awake long enough to have him breathe out the anesthesia. So I had a trampoline brought in and I would rebirth him while he was jumping on it. I'd say, "Lie down and breathe," until he would go asleep again and then I would put him back on the trampoline. It was very hard work, but he finally got through it.

Sometimes people who had anesthesia have thoughts like these:
- I can't get what I want.
- I can't make it.
- I am helpless.
- I need to be drugged in order to survive.
- I am immobile.
- Aliveness is terrifying.
- I have to deaden things or tone them down.
- I can't be in control of my own body.

Case Study 1: "My mother was happy to be totally anesthetized and feel no pain. She wasn't there for me; and the doctor had to use forceps because she could not push. As a result of this, I don't count on anyone or expect that anyone will give me anything. My main social defense mechanism is withdrawal. My social credo is that if people can't do anything good for each other, they can at least leave each other alone. When I was born I was very long, and my aunt, a nurse who was present, made sarcastic remarks. I have always been afraid of being made fun of, unwilling to do things I am afraid people will think are foolish, and I act aloof when I am really scared inside. I never bonded with my mother as she was out of it. I have been very emotionally cold and distant and never, until recently, have known what it was like to love another person."

Case Study 2: "My birth was easy—a typical hospital delivery. My mother was drugged with Twilight Sleep. She could see but not touch. A way my birth affects my relationships is that I've tried to be invisible to cover the hurt I felt about not being able to connect with my mother. My mother had the thought, "I am not here." I've felt disconnected and out of touch in many of my relationships. I tend to feel that I can't be with the people I love most, since at my birth I had to be around hospital personnel instead of my mom. And last, but not least, unconsciousness and spaciness—seem to be coming up strongly as I am writing this."

Affirmations for births with drugs:
- It is safe to be fully alive.
- I no longer need drugs to feel alive.
- My aliveness is a pleasure for me and everyone else.
- It is easy to be alive.
- It is safe to be in my body.
- It is safe to feel my feelings.
- It is safe to breathe fully and freely.
- I forgive my mother for being afraid of childbirth.
- I am safe to be with.
- It is safe to be intimate.
- I can express myself freely and fully.
- I no longer have to withhold to survive.
- It is safe to be fully out there!

There are many more birth types and conditions that we see, but are not covered here, including:
- transverse lie
- cord around the neck
- amniotic sac intact
- birth defects
- arm presentation
- RH factor
- twins, triplets, and quads
- implantation and modern methods of fertilization
- births in war zones, especially bombings during wars
- births during hurricanes, tornados, earthquakes, or natural disasters
- births during surprising catastrophes

- births in taxi cabs or cars
- births in elevators

Conscious Conception and Ideal Birth

The future of the human race is in the hands of our pregnant women! Even before pregnancy, one can read books such as *The Child of Your Dreams* by Laura Archera Huxley, which tells what you need to do to prepare for a *conscious conception*. Perhaps you know someone in your own family or circle of friends who is thinking about getting pregnant or who just got pregnant. You could do each woman a huge favor by exposing them to the best way to both prevent birth trauma and have an easier delivery.

We began with Dr. LeBoyer's research, which proved that babies born with the quiet birth are brighter, healthier, happier—even ambidextrous—and more joyful. *Who would not want this? What mother does not want to imagine she could have the whole birthing experience with a minimum of pain?* Then when I heard about the "Russian Method" of birth where mothers delivered the baby right into the water, it made total sense to me. The baby, who has already been living in fluid for nine months is simply released into a larger body of fluid and can integrate being outside of the mother first without having the shocking change of the atmosphere at the same time. Because the umbilical cord is still attached and pulsating, there is no danger of drowning.

As breathworkers, we recommend *conscious conception*. Imagine if a couple has already worked out their conception and birth trauma prior to conceiving a child! The higher the couples' consciousness can merge before and during conception, the nobler shall be the incoming soul. (Remember that the incoming child also chooses parents, heredity, the karma it will carry, and its path.) A matrix of perfection, like that which is found in a flawless diamond, must be held for the conceived child. The God Presence must be magnetized. To be a New Age parent, spiritual experiences must be protected so that the child can maintain its Godhead. *The children coming in now are higher than before, and we must be prepared for them.*

We cannot stress enough the importance of *conscious gestation* in which parents communicate directly with the fetus. The fetus should be reassured of parental love, respect, and joyful anticipation of birth. The pregnant woman can provide specific communications. For example, if she has an upset with someone, she can assure her unborn child, "It is alright, I am not mad at you. I forgive myself/him/her." As we have seen, intrauterine experiences that threaten a baby's wellbeing persist in memory and can have a lasting influence. Physician attitudes are crucial also, so one must choose the right delivery team.

Parents to be should read *The Secret Life of the Unborn Child* very early on. Dr. Thomas Verny explains that his findings have a profound implication for parents. He demonstrates that whether a child becomes happy or sad, aggressive or meek, secure or anxiety-ridden in later life depends in part on what messages the fetus received in the womb. The chief source of these messages is the mother; however, the father can have a significant positive or negative influence on the child's development as well. Prenatal psychology is a developing field and Dr. Verny is one of its pioneers.

We all need to think about how to create new generations that would lead humanity to a new society. In the mystic schools there was much emphasis on choosing the right mate in the first place. Marriage was considered a sacred friendship meant to bring in advanced souls. The couple had to be in service together and do daily worship. Certain meditations were given when it came to attracting an old soul. Old souls come to work as leaders, talents, and geniuses to further evolution. To attract those souls, the couple had to focus on higher planes and be in tune with each other like two musical instruments. They had to have great love, respect, and admiration. Great souls are attracted to great beauty. *Conscious conception* was considered a social responsibility. The mother to be should be surrounded by:

- beauty, nature, and the stars
- spiritual, uplifting, melodious music
- river, oceans, forests, and sounds of nature
- stories of great heroes
- Inspirations of faith

- forgiveness, love, and charity
- the best food available
- healthy people with high moral standards
- opportunities to engage in the arts
- peace
- abundance and security
- prayer and meditation

One of the most important books to read besides *The Secret Life of the Unborn Child* is *Education Begins before Birth* by the Master Omraam Mikhael Aivanhov, who brought the teachings of the Great White Brotherhood (ascended masters and enlightened mystics) to France. He talks always about the higher possibilities for the parents and the child. He makes it clear that to have the right to invite high spiritual entities into your aura to incarnate as your children, you must be fitted for the task. Superior beings will only agree to incarnate with parents who have already achieved a certain degree of purity and self-control. Even the angels should be invited in. He explains the importance of what he calls "spiritual gold plating" for the embryo which is related to having luminous thoughts.

It is ideal for both parents to be as enlightened as possible before conception of their baby. Imagine if a couple has been rebirthed and already worked out their own conception trauma and birth trauma prior to conception! The next best thing would be to do so before delivery.

Conscious Pregnancy and Childbirth

Women who experience Liberation Breathing® or rebirthing during pregnancy say their babies love it and they come out breathing a perfect conscious, connected breath! My colleague Eva Gundberg, M.D., Ph.D., author of *El Placer de Nacer* (*The Pleasure of Birth*), and President of The National Association for Prenatal Education in Venezuela has this to say:

"Mothers who have done rebirthing throughout their pregnancy have wonderful results. They seem to have calmer pregnancies, with babies who feel more secure in life. They have better births, fewer caesarian sections, and they want for birth what is fundamental—to be able to dilate and later to push. They feel strongly that they have the power to go through the process, and they feel a real satisfaction with the process when it's over. They make an intense connection with the baby and the husband in the post-partum and are excellent agents for change in the society, talking with passion about their birth and the importance of birthing."

Labor, delivery, and preparation for childbirth is a time when one has an enhanced opportunity to master one's environment and mind. The most important things for making the experience easier are:

- understanding the experience of using the Liberation Breathing® or rebirthing breath
- knowledge that you can instantly change each negative thought to the opposite in the form of an affirmation that will always reduce fear and pain
- faith
- a birth team you trust
- support from others you trust
- making the birthing space comfortable, beautiful, and relaxing
- massage
- high-vibration music
- a place to walk, dance, stretch, and move
- a general attitude of calmness and prayer

My mother amused herself when in labor with me by walking around the house whistling. A mother needs to remember that if she has a scary thought like "I can't do this," or "this is killing me," she has the opportunity in the next second to change her thought and get hold of her mind. Hanging on to the scary thoughts can make labor long and painful with a lot of suffering.

Affirmations for pregnancy and childbirth (from my book *Ideal Birth*):

- I am one with God.

- I am completely safe.
- I am completely safe in childbirth.
- Childbirth is safe and natural.
- The more I let go, the more relaxed I am and the less pain I have.
- Everything is happening perfectly.
- I am safe in God.
- I am safe and alive right now.
- I am life itself.
- I easily allow these symptoms to be absorbed by the energy that makes my body feel good.
- I feel great during my entire delivery.
- I let God manage all of it.
- I surrender completely to God.
- I allow this to be pleasurable.
- I am innocent and my baby is innocent.
- My contractions are pleasant expansions.
- I release all resistance.
- I do not resist God.
- I breathe fully and freely and let go.
- I am strong enough for this.
- God transmutes everything into love and pleasure.
- Childbirth brings more aliveness to me.

The affirmation I like to give women for delivery is: "My mind is God's Mind. I am One with God." *What would God's mind be like?* Imagine eternal bliss, love, all-knowing, joy, and peace. As long as a woman thinks she is separate from God, she will have guilt and create punishment in the form of pain. Pain is created by the ego mind because we have projected our ego onto God; we fear God. Because we fear God, we have not trusted God, and we have even made the mistake of thinking God kills people. *How then can you rely on God during labor?* I would suggest that a woman in labor has someone read from *A Course in Miracles* out loud. Women who read my book *Ideal Birth* wrote and thanked me for the *A*

Course in Miracles lessons I had suggested for labor. Here they are from the *Workbook for Students*:
- Lesson 29: God is in everything I see.
- Lesson 34: I could see peace instead of this.
- Lesson 42: God is My Strength. Vision is His Gift.
- Lesson 45: God is the Mind with which I think.
- Lesson 47: God is the strength in which I trust.
- Lesson 101: God's will for me is perfect happiness.
- Lesson 124: Let me remember that I am one with God.
- Lesson 162: I am as God Created me.
- Lesson 163: There is no death. The Son of God is free.
- Lesson 164: Now we are one with Him who is our Source.
- Lesson 165: Let not my mind deny the thought of God.
- Lesson 185: I want the Peace of God.
- Lesson 190: I choose the joy of God instead of pain.
- Lesson 240: Fear is not justified in any form.
- Lesson 244: I am in danger nowhere in the world.

Optimizing the Post-Natal Experience

After birth the baby and mother should not be separated. Author and birthing expert, Suzanne Arms (Birthing the Future), in a prenatal conference I attended, stated the following: "Immediate separation after delivery deprives both the mother and child of their greatest opportunity for emotional bonding. This lack, when the baby is separated, undermines trust, and many babies spend the rest of their lives regaining trust." The manner in which a society greets its newborn members has a lot to do with the shaping of the newborn's overall character. Failure to develop peaceful behaviors begins during childbirth due to lack of bonding and impersonal practices.

I have facilitated breathing sessions with many people who felt that their father did not hold them at all when they were infants. The women especially grew up feeling "untouched" by a man and made many unconscious decisions about that. Later in life, the men they loved the most would not touch them. They then became bitter and resentful against their mates and this resulted in even less touching.

There can never be too much holding of a newborn. Body contact and touch is the most important thing of all. In the field of anthropology, research shows that tribes with the most confident, strong, secure beings are those in which babies are carried everywhere, next to the mother at all times. Breastfeeding is done often and on demand. The more activity the mother has while the baby is next to her body, the better. Jean Liedloff in *The Continuum Concept* notes that a mother sitting still all the time will condition the baby to think life is dull, and if the mother treats the baby as fragile, it will be

Below are suggestions I have written for optimizing the postnatal experience:
- arrival into lots of warm pleasure (such as underwater birth)
- soft lights, warm room, music playing
- chants and prayers
- flowers, candles, crystals
- midwives who are extremely loving, positive, breathing well, and have cleared their birth trauma (who understand the principles of this book)
- present father
- family and friends with whom the parents feel clear
- periods of silence for receiving communication from the baby
- frequent and meaningful eye-to-eye contact
- smiling
- soothing sounds and words
- Speaking in affirmations and certainty (verbally or non-verbally)
- gentle warm touch including carrying and close body contact
- spiritual teacher, spiritual healer, or energy channel
- masseuse who knows how to do baby massage
- cranial therapist
- atmosphere of celebration without raucous energy
- well prepared siblings
- gifts beautifully wrapped

- gifts of money to develop immediate prosperity consciousness (remember the baby is really many lifetimes old, and knows what is going on)

Parents should immediately release guilt if the birth did not turn out according to the birth plan. When a baby is born there are multiple people involved: the father (and his birth script), the mother (and her birth script), the birth team (and their birth scripts), as well as the baby's karma. Babies often "create" a birth related to previous past lives. The book *Other Lives, Other Selves* by Dr. Roger Woolger is a good source of information. Every child comes out the way he or she is supposed to, after all.

Latest Ideas about Birth

Markus and I had the pleasure of spending some time with my friend Dr. Michel Odent when he was in Hawaii. His latest book is *Childbirth and The Future of Homo Sapiens*. He is the clearest person I know about how reducing birth trauma affects humanity. He was the first Obstetrician to write about underwater birth in medicine. He stressed to us the importance of utilizing the natural oxytocin, which is the love hormone that peaks moments after birth and causes overwhelming love and bliss. Nothing, and he means nothing, should interfere with this. So, he says, women should birth privately with the midwife sitting in the corner knitting. (This is so she does not transmit her adrenaline to contaminate the space). After the birth itself, the baby should be skin to skin with the mother immediately, instead of being wiped off. He even claims that the father should be in the kitchen with the Obstetrician talking, because births should not be "masculinized." Dr. Odent says, "Try to imagine what would happen if we tried to snatch a newborn from the arms of a gorilla. Right after birth the woman is at her most powerful." He says socializing birth neutralizes this force.

The Divine Mother of Birth in Bali—Robin Lim

Markus and I had the privilege of meeting Robin Lim in Bali after she was named the 2011 CNN Hero of the Year. She is an American who has helped thousands of poor Indonesian women to have healthy pregnancies and deliveries. She offers free prenatal care, birthing services, and medical aid. She wants every baby's first breath to be peace and love. She started the "Healthy Mother Earth Foundation" officially known as Yayasan Bumi Sehat. We visited her Bumi Sehat Clinic where underwater birth and delayed cutting of the umbilical cord are offered. This, she says, produces healthier more intelligent youngsters. She calls her gentle birthing method *Wisdom Birth*.

Lim has written three books: *After the Baby's Birth, Eating for Two,* and *Placenta: The Forgotten Chakra*. The latter documents an increase in mother-baby bonding and baby's better emotional health when the cutting of the cord is delayed. I can honestly say that my friend Robin is a real angel to the people. This was obvious to us when we saw how much everyone loved her.

In Bali, children are blessed through many important ceremonies. At 7-8 months of the pregnancy, a ceremony is performed to ensure the wellbeing and health of the infant and to ask for blessings of an easy birth. After the birth, there are a series of ceremonies through which the mother and baby are purified. The amazing thing is that the babies are carried and kept next to the bodies of the parents for three whole months!! Nor do they leave the family compound. At three months there is a "grounding ceremony" attended by relatives and neighbors. This is performed by the Priest of the family, who re-introduces the child to the world. Then the baby's feet will touch the ground for the first time. The baby is also held over a flat clay bowl which contains items representing intelligence, wisdom, wealth, industriousness, and diligence. I am convinced that this process results in tremendous self-esteem, freedom from fear, and other wonderful qualities. The Balinese are very peaceful, calm, and marvelous to behold.

A Tribute to My Mother

From the very beginning my mother really wanted me. I love that I was wanted and planned. She told everyone in our little town, *"This is the year!"* My mom was so tuned in to me in the womb that she actually got my telepathic request: I wanted to be born at home (which was highly unusual back then). My older sister had been born in the hospital. It was expected and popular to have a hospital birth. Because my mother was careful to bond with me prenatally, and to communicate with me, she acknowledged my desires as a being. I wanted to be born at home no matter what. (In many breathing sessions I have actually remembered trying to communicate this to her from the womb. She got it and I appreciated it.)

During the labor, my mom walked around the house a lot and actually whistled during the contractions. This was more comfortable for me because it relaxed her. To this day, I go into bliss when I hear someone whistle.

At my delivery I had both a family doctor and a midwife, who was my mom's best friend. The problem was this: the midwife had been my father's high school sweetheart and she was waiting for my Dad to come home from college and marry *her*. Instead, he brought back a Swedish woman, Ethel Ingeborg, my mother. The midwife had a fit of jealousy come up at my birth wanting me to be her baby with my Dad. My mom and she even got in an argument over my name. My Dad was there, but this was too much for him, so he went out on the porch and had a cigarette. I pulled back to wait for him to return and he did not. This screwed up my birth. I spent years "waiting" for things—especially men.

My birth was a very social event. I have always been, as a result, a very social person. I had no drugs, so I came out wide awake and happy. After birth I had the immediate benefit of being with my mother all the time without interruption. I was not taken to a nursery and I did not have to go through "separation anxiety." I feel this greatly contributed to my self-esteem and resulting success. The only drawback was that everyone in town came to see me right away, so I got no break and I became a public figure immediately.

I loved the way my mother reared me. When I was a child she gave me total space. I felt free to grow up without a lot of heavy rules, disapproval, or strict discipline. I did not need discipline; what I needed was a good example and she gave me that. My mother always trusted me completely and I felt that at all times. She seemed to be saying telepathically, from the beginning, "I trust you. You are good and I know you know what you are doing. I give you space to be yourself." I felt this at a very early age and as a result, I wanted to live up to her highest thoughts about me. I wanted never to disappoint her high opinion of me. I was a good child, eager to be a responsible being like she was.

My mother allowed me to be different—perhaps my greatest blessing of all. She just prayed for me and gave me unconditional love. I do not remember my mother ever complaining. I do not remember my parents ever fighting. In fact, they had an agreement never to raise their voices in my presence and they never did. This I appreciate more than you can imagine. My mother always thought positively and let go of any upset so fast I did not even notice. She taught me literally how to go to higher thoughts.

She always had faith in me, and that worked. She acted as if I could take care of myself so she was never guilty of over parenting. This enabled me to be very expressive and creative and to feel happy and free. I must admit I was raised in a very small town and everyone knew where I belonged and parented me if I needed it, wherever I was. I was lucky. My big sadness was that my father was sick and in and out of hospitals my whole childhood. Liberation Breathing® healed me of that also.

Part 8

Ascension and Physical Immortality

The Unconscious Death Urge

What is the unconscious death urge? It is a conglomerate in the unconscious mind that includes the following thoughts:
- I am separate from God
- death is inevitable
- belief in one's personal lie
- all anti-life thoughts
- family traditions on death (what your ancestors died of)
- false religious theology
- all guilt
- the belief in sin
- the secret wish to die if you dislike your life
- past life memories of dying

You can tell when your death urge is up by the way you feel and by the way things are going in your life. Sickness, depression, lack of energy or lack of motivation are all results of the death urge. If things are falling apart around you, i.e., plants dying, car dying, pets dying, or relationships going dead, that is also the unconscious death urge showing up in your space. Your death urge will likely get activated when a friend or family member dies. Failure in business or a divorce can trigger the death urge. This is when Liberation Breathing® sessions can be most beneficial.

The results of the death urge are:
- fear
- sapped vitality and fatigue
- lack of clarity
- inhibited creativity
- illness
- aging
- blocked wisdom
- anger
- depression

- helplessness
- failure, loss of money, etc.
- anything not working in your space
- warfare (social statement of the group death urge)

We have a saying that goes like this: "*The death urge keeps out the love that would heal it.*" This means that when your death urge is up you tend to push away love and support, which is exactly what you need. Become aware of this trick of the ego, and push through it by asking for support, even when you might want to avoid it. Avoiding support usually results in becoming stuck.

I had a client who was devastated by the end of a relationship. She came to me wanting to die and kill herself because she was all alone on her birthday and no roses arrived from him. None of her friends came through either. She was feeling that she did not matter, and asking, "What was the use?" She felt so dead that at the beginning of the session she felt nothing and breathing was not working.

I prayed like mad how to help this woman, and I was instructed to put on the anti-death mantra:

> Om Tryambakam Yajaamahe
> Sugandhim Pushti Vardhanam
> Urvaar Rukamiva Bandhanaan
> Mrityor Mukshiya Mamritaat

When the music started, her breathing changed and she finally felt some energy. She kept breathing and breathing until she got to the place where she wanted to live again. I was very clear that if she had not come for a session, she might have gotten very sick or had a car accident. She was aware of that too. Another miracle!

Here are the causes of aging and death:

- Invalidation of your personal divinity (such as indulging in personal lie)
- False religious theology (such as sin is real, you are separate from God, and death is inevitable)
- Lack of immortalist philosophy (nobody ever taught you the truth)

- False belief systems (medical beliefs that at age "70" such and such will happen)
- Family traditions around death (my grandfather died at 85, therefore, I probably will too)
- Addictions and overeating
- Anger and non-forgiveness
- Unresolved tension and unresolved birth trauma
- Anger at God
- Unconscious death urge

No shot or elixir will process your unconscious death urge. This is a spiritual matter. Spiritual purification clears the death urge. You weaken the soul's harmonic habitation of the body with thoughts like "death is inevitable" and "disease is stronger than the power of God."

Aging is controlled by consciousness. Aging is programming. Aging indicates the body is not being allowed to clear itself. When the body cannot clear itself, the body dies. That is why we use Liberation Breathing® to clear the body. *Free your body from the orders you laid upon it.* In other words, command yourself to live rather than to die. The ability to lead a long life comes when the body is not forced to do what it does not want to do.

An Outline of My Spiritual Healing Course

Much of this I learned from dedicated study of *A Course in Miracles*. Some of it I learned from my many spiritual teachers. Some of it I learned from my research as a breathworker watching thousands healed by the breath. Very little of it I learned in medicine. Working with a LB® practitioner can help you will feel the way you always wanted to feel.

I. You will be healed when you see no more value in pain and symptoms.
   A. You have to be willing to give up the "payoff." (neurotic benefits)
   B. Sickness is a decision—an election—you choose it.

C. *A Course in Miracles* says that all illness is mental illness and the mind is off.
D. The *Course* says that you are "trying to kill God."
E. Healing can be a threat because you are responsible for your thoughts.
F. To heal, you must say, "There is no gain in this."

II. The physician is the mind of the patient himself.
   A. The outcome is what the patient decides himself.
   B. Special agents (pills, etc.) only give form to the patient's desires. They are not actually needed at all.
   C. The mind rules the body in all cases.
   D. Most people believe that their sickness has chosen them. This is false.
   E. Sickness is not an accident. It is an insane device for self-deception. Its purpose is to hide reality—to keep you from seeing what you need to see. You can't heal it permanently until you take responsibility for creating it. You may resist doing this. (There is a tendency to attack what does not satisfy you to avoid seeing that you created it.) This is a trick of the ego and you have to catch it.

III. Facing your pain
   A. All pain is the effort involved in clinging to a negative thought (ego).
   B. In pain, God is denied and fear is triumphing.
   C. Pain is sleep, is ego (fear), is wrong perspective—a sign illusions are reigning.
   D. It is your thoughts alone that cause you pain. Nothing external can hurt you and no one but yourself affects you.
   E. Pain is fear. Fear is denying love. Denying love is using pain to prove that God is dead.
   F. The body can act wrongly only when it is responding to wrong thoughts. The body cannot create; it is a result, not a cause.

IV. Facing the fear of healing
   A. Sudden healing could produce depression in people who have chosen sickness as a way of life and a major way of getting attention.
   B. Do not pray for a miracle healing overnight (of your cancer for example). You probably could not accept it, because it would change your reality so quickly that it would produce fear.
   C. The Holy Spirit will never add to your fear.
   D. Pray for the removal of the fear of healing first, then of the conditions that produced the fear.
      1. Every time you give up something negative you get more energy and more of God. That is what people are really afraid of.
      2. We are all used to and addicted to misery, pain, conflict, and death. In other words, we have grown accustomed to hell.
      3. What we are really afraid of is the unfamiliar: peace, more life, more God, more love, and more energy.
      4. So we tend to hang on to a condition (sickness, pain, or any problem) that brings us down because we fear getting higher (God). We do this because we are so confused from the church that we think God kills people…so we better not have more of God! This keeps us stuck.
   E. You have to stop pretending that sickness and pain are accidents. You have to stop pretending that you do not make them up.
      1. You see an imagined threat (illusion) which you make real, and then you make up a defense (sickness, symptoms, or pain), and then you pretend that you did not do that and it is all beyond your control.
      2. Then you are mad at God because you feel lousy. Again, you attack what does not satisfy you to avoid seeing that you made it up.
      3. You have to stop this insanity and see that it is a useless game. It is a plan to defeat what cannot be attacked (God and life).
      4. The whole useless game keeps the mind split between being a victim and being responsible.
      5. Even killing yourself to get out of pain is no solution. Death is no solution. Consciousness, when departing the body, automatically

seeks its own level. In other words, you will keep the same mental conditions that made the illness until you look at it and release it.
6. You may hate God because you are sick and in pain, but I assure you that the reason you are sick or in pain is because you hate God.
7. Liberation Breathing® is a simple, wonderful way of healing yourself. Since it is conscious breathing and is pulling in the Spirit on the inhale, and releasing the ego (negative thoughts) on the exhale, you can literally pump out all thoughts that made you sick.

V. Healing will flash across an open mind
   A. All healing is temporary until you heal death.
   B. We could teach you how to heal anything with your mind, including cancer, but if you don't give up your death urge, you will just make up a new way to kill yourself.
   C. As long as you think, "Death is inevitable," you will have to create some sickness to prove you are right.
   D. The *Course* says, "And death is the result of the thought we call the ego, as surely as life is the result of the Thought of God." (T 19 IV. 2:15)
   E. Are you going to choose the ego and try to kill God? It won't work. There is no escape from your own consciousness!

VI. The Atonement heals with certainty
   A. Say "I am one with God and I allow the Holy Spirit to undo all my wrong thinking." (This is the Atonement.)
   B. The Atonement cures all sickness. It takes away the guilt that made the sickness.
   C. "Only salvation can be said to cure." (WB Lesson 140). "Atonement heals with certainty, and cures all sickness. The mind which understands that sickness can be nothing but a dream is not deceived by forms the dream may take. Sickness where guilt is absent cannot come, for it is but another form of guilt. Atonement does not heal the sick, for that is not a cure. It takes away the guilt that makes the sickness possible. And that

is cure indeed. For sickness now is gone, with nothing left to which it can return."

D. Atonement is the relinquishment of all your judgments, attack thoughts, grievances, anger, and basically all thoughts that do not make you supremely happy. It is the attainment of Christ's Vision of a completely "forgiven world." It is the total stepping out of the thought system of the ego, one "separated" from its divine Source and ruled by the fear of separation, punishment and guilt… into the Thought of God, which is your true Identity imbued with innocence, wholeness and light in which you were originally created. Through complete forgiveness Atonement is reached; in the state of Atonement awareness of Self-Identity is attained; in the extension of Atonement does one fulfill their divine purpose and mission in life, living solely in the perfect happiness of Divine Grace. It is the main job of Jesus in *A Course in Miracles* to awaken us to this state of Self-Identity through Atonement; He even states: "I am in charge of the process of Atonement, which I undertook to begin." (T1 III. 1:1) So, Christ's Vision [of complete forgiveness] is the means for us to realize this state of being, and to extend it to others in our lives.

E. The sole responsibility you have to produce miracles is to accept the Atonement for yourself.

F. To heal is to make happy. You have had many opportunities to gladden yourself and you have refused them.

G. All forms of sickness and death are physical expressions of the fear you have of awakening. They are attempts to reinforce sleeping. Sleep is withdrawing…a form of death. Death is unconsciousness.

H. Healing is release from fear of awakening. All healing involves waking up and replacing fear with love, guilt with innocence.

"'There is a Spirit in man: the inspiration of the Almighty giveth him understanding,' says Job. This Spirit in man is his God. The inspiration is his breath of God. The God within and the God without are united by breathing. But the external breath of air into the lungs is only a symbol, a hint of the true breath, which right thoughts can give, if they are put forth and taken in at the moment of intense experience. It is equally powerful if in a moment of great joy one keeps firmly to the same great TRUTH. Firmness is poise, balance of character. This is a great healing quality. We become healers of disease according to our poise of character."

—Emma C. Hopkins, *Scientific Christian Mental Practice* (p. 82)

VII. Spiritual healing has three steps which proceed from a poised character:
    A. Find the cause (which are always preceding thoughts/memories)
        1. To find the cause you have to locate the negative thoughts that caused the condition in the first place. You have to find your most negative thought about your body and your most negative thought about life. You have to find out what your payoff is for keeping the condition and what is your fear of giving it up.
    B. Confession (which is taking 100% responsibility for this "cause")
        1. For the confession part you need to confess to God, a partner, friend or for sure to your Liberation Breathing® breathworker what these thoughts are/were.
    C. Spiritual purification practices bring in the Divine Energy for cleansing, healing, and release of thoughts
        1. Spiritual purification practices could include Liberation Breathing® / Prayer / Ho'Oponopono / Yoga / Affirmations / Chanting / Fire purification / Practicing *A Course in Miracles* Lessons / Sweat Lodge / Body Work such as deep tissue body work or Rolfing / Cranial-Sacral Work / and perhaps even a Mundun (head shaving)! These are just a few practices.

The Path of Ascension

Life is the highest force in the universe. The way of everlasting life is a sacrament offered to all. I always feel honored when I am asked to speak on the subject of ascension and physical immortality. I feel like I am speaking about the highest blessing.

Death has been a popular habit for about 4,500 years. Before that, Masters lived to be 400-5,000 years old. This is recorded in texts in India. In the Bible, immortal Masters including Melchizedek, Enoch, and Elijah are mentioned, but people seem to forget that. By practicing the spiritual laws of enlightenment, you can become a Master yourself. Jesus acknowledges this.

I usually don't teach this subject without clearing people on religious dogma first because they get stuck. While religious dogma teaches that "death is inevitable," the Bible talks about immortal Masters. What a *contradiction*. No wonder everyone experiences confusion. That is why we teach *A Course in Miracles* before teaching physical immortality and ascension.

A Course in Miracles teaches: "Death is not your Father's will, nor yours." The *Course* says, "The death penalty is the ego's ultimate goal, for it truly believes that you are a criminal, as deserving of death as God knows you are deserving of life. The death penalty never leaves the ego's mind for that is what it always reserves for you in the end…It will torment you while you live; but its hatred is not satisfied until you die" (T12 VII 13:2-5). Remember this: Jesus did not die. *Why would eternal life be given to only one of God's sons?* When you learn to manifest Christ consciousness in yourself, you will never want or see death. *A Course in Miracles* explains repeatedly that no one dies unless he chooses death.

The purpose of this initiation is never to glorify the body. The purpose of achieving ascension and physical immortality is to stay alive so that you can do a mission of Divine Service that the Masters ask you to do. *How can you do your mission when you are sick or decrepit?* Personally, it took me so long to clear myself that I feel my true wisdom is really coming forth and it would be a waste if I started checking out now, just when I can really make a difference. You may think you don't have a mission, but maybe you just never tuned into the Divine Plan of your life. Your mission could start any minute.

Ascension and the Role of Liberation Breathing

To ascend the ladder of holiness and truth toward the light, which is also toward our own light, is our reason for being. Yoga is a practice of ascension. Pranayama helps one ascend. *A Course in Miracles* offers a path of ascension. Ho'oponopono provides a tool for ascension. And Liberation Breathing® from the Divine Mother is a path of ascension, which integrates all of the above. Humankind for eons has aspired to higher levels of truth and beauty within the physical context of daily existence. Heaven on earth is a noble aspiration, and this ever-widening potential has gripped the human psyche in its effort to ascend and attain this level of enlightenment of the spirit.

"The Kingdom of Heaven is within you" are words ascribed to Jesus in the Bible. In *A Course in Miracles*, Jesus tells us "the Kingdom of Heaven *is* you." He says, "It is hard to understand what 'the Kingdom of Heaven is within you' really means. This is because it is not understandable to the ego, which interprets it as if something outside is inside, and this does not mean anything. The word 'within' is unnecessary. The Kingdom of Heaven *is* you. What else *but* you did the Creator create, and what else *but* you is His Kingdom?" (*A Course in Miracles* T4, III:1-5)

Ascension is merely the full realization of who I am as God created me. It is the realization that I am the Kingdom of Heaven *now*. It is an outgrowing process of all lower levels of thought "identification" in which awareness of who I am ascends beyond problems, guilt, sin, shame, anger, pain, disease, and even death. I see my true identity at the undaunted level of the Spirit. In this ascended state of mind, the reality of grace and beauty engulfs me. Intense and profound gratitude becomes my daily truth.

The sages of old knew this fact of our inherent innocence. They did not foster a belief in original sin. The shining Beings of the Age of Truth were certain of their light, and clear that their purpose on this earth was to bless creation with the awareness of Divine Joy. They participated in creation to extend this Truth and Joy. Light, love, and beauty composed their source. Grace was their function to extend. Liberation Breathing® is the link we aspire to use for our return to our original identity we share with them. Creation Herself gives us the gift of life, of breath. It is the blessing of a loving Divine Mother to her children of love. On the path of ascension leading to full self-realization, Liberation Breathing® plays an essential role in our return to Love, which is who we are.

The advantages to being on the path of ascension include increased:
- health
- energy
- creativity
- quality of life
- potential for regeneration
- intelligence
- fun
- joy

Imagine feeling better than you have ever felt in your life. Imagine living fully without any control. Life without death is pure life!

When you are on the ascension path, it is a progressive movement into divine truth. It comes in stages. You are continuously raising your vibrational frequency. You are continually getting more and more light. You go through the death of the ego, while ascending the ladder of Holiness. You grow into the Christ Mind and the Christ Body. You achieve mind-body mastery by staying in a state of love, praise, and gratitude. A well-trained LB® practitioner knows how to help you with this process. Babaji has given me mantras for longevity and physical immortality and ascension. I can teach you these. They are very powerful and are not to be entrusted to the non-serious. I can also lead you to other immortalists who have more knowledge than I do. You can learn to translate your body. Being on the ascension path is the highest path. You rise up to the highest dimensions.

Physical Immortality

Physical immortality can be defined as endless existence, specifically the endless existence of your physical body in perpetual health and youthfulness.

The belief that death is inevitable has killed more people than any other cause. There are case histories of people living for thousands of years by practicing simple spiritual purification, but you would never think of looking for them if you didn't believe in the possibility of physical immortality. If you understand the truth that your thoughts create your reality and you have certain knowledge of that, then taking it all the way, you will see that what happens to your body is also the result of your thoughts. The trouble is, we all "bought into" the popular belief that you have to die around 70. (A belief is just a group of thoughts.) There are people around who have lived a lot longer. There are even people walking around who look 30 and are actually much, much older. Some could be in their hundreds; but they are not going to tell the truth about that yet. It is not safe for them to do so. (Read about St. Germaine for example.)

Jesus conquered death and that was the whole point of the New Testament. He was showing you could master your body when you conquer your ego. He passed his initiation! Few got it. Most people got stuck on the crucifixion and missed the point of the Resurrection. If you read what he says in *A Course in Miracles*, he explains that the crucifixion was an extreme teaching device to show you that there are no victims. Jesus took his body with him. He materializes it for certain devotees even now. As I said previously, Babaji materialized his body for fourteen years to heal us in the coming time of strife. He has materialized and de-materialized his body at will for thousands of years. You can read about him in Yogananda's book, *Autobiography of a Yogi*, and Leonard Orr's books *Physical Immortality: The Science of Everlasting Life*, and his newer book *Breaking the Death Habit*.

The main point I want to make is that you do have a *choice* about what to do with your body. Jesus said, "The power of life and death are in the tongue."

It is essential to look at the issue of death and physical immortality if you are starting the breathing process. Leonard always taught us that it is unethical to teach enlightenment to our clients and students without teaching them how death works. This is absolutely the truth and one should make sure one's practitioner has had the proper training on this issue.

The reason is this: As you become more enlightened and change your negative thoughts to positive thoughts, you get more energy. As you rebirth and do conscious breathing, you add even more power and energy to your thoughts. You end up with a lot more spiritual force behind your thoughts. That means your thoughts will manifest more quickly. If you hang onto the thought "death is inevitable" and keep breathing consciously, you will have a lot more force behind *that* thought. Since what you think about expands, your death urge would increase and you could kill yourself faster! Surely the purpose of enlightenment and Liberation Breathing is *not* so you can kill yourself faster! This is why it is imperative that your practitioner helps you change *all* your negative thoughts.

Even the thought "death is inevitable" is just a thought. But you say, "I see everyone dying out there all the time so I know it is real." Think again. All those people who are dying killed themselves with that belief and other anti-life thoughts. They never learned thought is creative. Again, the truth is *all death is suicide*. People kill themselves with their own thoughts. The body dies when it can no longer clear itself of the conglomerate of negative thoughts and memories. Please get this point: we now have a technique of clearing the mind and body. You can clear yourself of this negative conditioning around death with Liberation Breathing and rebirthing.

People often say to me, "Oh I would never want to live forever. It is too much pain and misery." Of course you wouldn't! I am not talking about living in pain and misery. But the reason you are in pain and misery is that you have not cleared the death urge. I am not talking about living in an old decrepit body either. *Who would want that?*

I am talking about staying the age you want, looking and feeling good, and staying that way. If you could have *that*, then you might want to stick around. You can have that (the Fountain of Youth) if you will surrender to these ideas, change your thoughts and experience to *youthing*. If you stay on the path of ascension (constantly raising the vibrations of your mind and body to more and more light), there is a point where you actually do stop aging! Please read this sentence again.

If you stay on the path of ascension (constantly raising the vibrations of your mind and body to more and more light), there is a point where you actually do stop aging!

I do not pretend to know the highest thought of how the body will look after mastering the mind and body. I do know that the masters call it claiming your diamond Christ Body. From her book *The Door of Everything*, Ruby Nelson writes:

"The last and greatest evil to be removed from the precious planet earth is Satan's evil death. Jesus said, 'Verily, verily I say unto you, if a man keep my word, he shall never see death.' Could any talk be plainer? It is true that life is everlasting regardless of how many times one lets the body die. It is true that the soul lives on and can create a new body for itself (reincarnation if you choose). But, it is also true that the soul is endowed with wisdom and it knows death of the body is out of harmony with the universal law of life. The soul yearns to be exalted to vibration of the ascension attitudes (love, praise, and gratitude) so it can travel the way of saints. In order to travel this highway, it needs a body which overcomes the destructive earth vibrations and is transmutable into light (dematerializing and rematerializing).

"When one chooses to die, death does release the weight of gravity and temporarily frees the soul from earth. But it does not change the vibrations of consciousness from the human level. [In other words, you do not go to a higher plane automatically where you are better off.]

"*There is no escape from the vibration of yourself* except by practiced change of thoughts. Nor does death cause the released consciousness to go to a celestial level. Consciousness, when departing from the body, automatically seeks is own level."

So there you are, right where you left off in this life anyway. It is better to get as enlightened as possible now!

"Every lifetime is a new opportunity," Nelson says, "to be enlightened and anointed with the light and rise above the trap of death…For he that is joined to Him that is immortal, will also himself become immortal" (from the chapter "The Lightening Flash").

The great news about living today is that the build up to 2012 has allowed us to make thousands of years of spiritual progress in one year. Get that: it would have taken us thousands of years before. There was a portal that opened during Harmonic Convergence and it built up to 2012. Further, my Rolfer in Nashville told me that if one can just stay young for the next 15 years, science itself will by then know how to keep the body from aging. Science is catching up to the spiritual masters.

One has to break out of the habit of dying and reincarnating. You can finally get to one lifetime where reincarnation becomes obsolete and you become a spiritual master. *Is it time for you?* Once you have worked out your birth trauma from your consciousness, why go through another birth trauma and go through it all again? Do you really want another birth trauma, another set of parents, another set of diapers, another school system, another church dogma, and another calculus class?

You have to love your body as much as God loves the earth. The experience of eternal love of your temple (body) will ultimately turn your body into light vibration and there will be transmutation of the cells (a "quickening" as they say in the Bible) to the point that one day you can have a saint-like body through transmutation.

It is important to realize that you are *not* simply your body. Your body is in *you*, the greater self. The body is a reflection of your thought forms and held together by a thought. The vibratory rate of the cells is slowed down enough for you to be seen. When you dematerialize, you increase the vibratory rate of cells enough to make them move into the One.

A yogi once taught me the following version of physical immortality:
- Spirit is that which cannot be destroyed.
- Mind is condensed Spirit.
- Body is condensed mind.
- Therefore the body is utmost Spirit.

If you can understand and believe that, physical immortality makes sense. Most people think they are separate from Spirit because they have been taught they are separate from God. This misperception leads to death. You cannot separate yourself from God. Impossible! *A Course in Miracles* says that the only thing we need to correct is our *imagined* separation from God. The *Course* is a correction of religion and wants to correct that sense of separation. It is the main issue.

When there is a lie at the center of a thought system, such as in religion, the whole thing is deceptive. The lie at the center of most religious dogma is that you are separate from God. You have to undo a lot of false religious theology to understand this. You are a cell in God's body. You are like a piece of pie and the whole pie is God. When you, one piece, are taken out of the pie tin and placed on a plate…it is only an illusion that it is separated. It is still pie!

Even if you do want to kill off your body with those kinds of thoughts, your soul cannot die. Therefore you will be left with yourself (your same consciousness) without a body, and you will have to reincarnate and try it all again. I hope you get it in this incarnation and choose the path of ascension. If you don't, at least you are sowing the seeds of mastery in your consciousness for the next time.

This would be like my organizer in Milano, Michelangelo. My guru Shastriji (Babaji's High Priest) told me that Michelangelo would make it as an immortal in this life and that he had been trying for many lifetimes. He is going to pass his initiation this time!

There is an alternative to death; and it is possible to go on living forever without dropping your body! Physical immortality, perpetual longevity, eternal life in your living flesh is now a practical possibility. There is also an alternative to aging. The habit of affirming the power of death causes not only death, but also many illnesses and the aging process itself. Many people are determined to die to maintain the tradition of death.

Most people want proof that it is possible to go on living without dropping your body. I did, in fact, meet a 400 year-old female in India, but I know the only reason I was allowed to meet her was because I did not have a doubt. I did not need to see it to believe it. I had already studied about the immortal masters and she knew that. *Why would she want a lot of people with doubt bothering her? If you need proof, the only possible proof would be to live forever, and who can measure forever?* This chapter could be read as an exercise for you…like a *koan*…a saying you can't figure out but is nevertheless captivating and true.

From a practical standpoint however, accepting the philosophy of physical immortality has at least as much benefit as having a *deathist* mentality. And it would be a lot better for the health of your mind, body, and spirit!

The idea of physical immortality may sound new, but it has been around since literature began. Spiritual masters of all religious have taught these ideas for centuries. You may have heard stories about these masters; but maybe you felt they were myths.

The Bible tells us that Enoch, the father of Methuselah, was the first man to conquer death. He lived thousands of years before Jesus. Elijah lived several centuries before Jesus and conquered death. Elijah actually materialized in the air to an immortalist friend of mine, Robert Coon (see his web site). For four hours Elijah transmitted telepathically to Robert the knowledge of physical immortality.

Alan Harrington in *The Immortalist* says that humans have always hated God for putting them in a closed universe from which they cannot escape alive. God did not do that. Suppressed anger at God will kill you too. Stanley Spears in *Stop Dying and Live Forever* uses the phrase, "Death is a grave mistake."

Why would God want to destroy after seventy years something that took millions of years to evolve? The truth is that the same Infinite Intelligence that evolved your physical body knows what to do to protect your body from whatever you *think* kills it. It is your mind that creates the death of your body. If you think you are going to die then you will.

I remember reading about the man who has lived longer from AIDS than anyone else in the world. They study him all the time trying to figure out what it is about him: *meditation? food? what practice?* In an article among all of the questions, he himself explained that when he got the diagnosis, he went home and told his mate, "I am *not* going to die!" Even the person who wrote the article, however, did not get the connection.

Leonard Orr coined the term *youthing*, the opposite of aging. Your body has the ability to produce new cells. For example, when you cut yourself, your body builds brand new cells to repair the cut. You know this. Scientific theory tells us that the body totally renews itself every eleven months! Your body is a constantly flowing stream of life. The cells are constantly changing, and the fact is that your mind is the only element that *ages*. The mind creates older *new* cells that correspond to the beliefs programmed into it. We have several alternatives when it comes to producing cells.

- Cells reproduce themselves exactly the same as they were.
- Cells reproduce themselves worse.
- Cells reproduce themselves better.
- Cells don't reproduce themselves.
- New cells are produced that you never had before.

If you are producing scar tissue cells, you are producing cells that turn out worse than the original ones. If you are losing weight, you are not producing new cells. If you are gaining weight then you are producing new cells. *Isn't it amazing?* Our mind controls which alternative works and which part of the body is affected. Consider the possibilities you have in controlling the cells you reproduce. You can flow your stream of life in either direction—youthing or aging.

One woman I know read the book *Rebirthing in The New Age* that Leonard and I wrote. She decided to reverse her menopause and have a baby with her new man. She did it. She traveled a long way in Europe to come and meet me and we both cried.

Bruce Lipton, scientist, biologist, wrote in the book *Biology of Belief* that he discovered our cells are innately intelligent and that they are akin to liquid crystal microchips, which receive and process information from the environment, thoughts, and beliefs. It follows then that we can reprogram ourselves!

The three aspects to developing physical immortality are:

Develop the *philosophy* of physical immortality.
- Get your mind and body in harmony with the Eternal Spirit.
- Read immortalist literature (see reading list in back of this book).

- Attend or listen to lectures on the subject (i.e. "Unraveling the Birth/Death Cycle" by Leonard Orr).

Develop the *psychology* of physical immortality.
- Unravel your personal death urge.
- Study your family traditions.
- Find out how your ancestors died and at what age. Choose not to copy them. Unless your parents were immortal yogis, you inherited a death urge. This personal death urge will kill you unless you kill it. You kill it by unraveling all your programming. Death has no power except that which you give it in your own mind. Nobody can kill you but you without your consent. Life is stronger than death.

Develop the *physiology* of physical immortality.
- Study and experience breath mastery through Liberation Breathing®. Get body treatments (rolfing, chiropractic, acupuncture, etc.).
- Master food and sleep.
- Reduce sleep and reduce food. Experiment with fasting.
- Adjust your belief system about food; there are even breatharians who live on the light of God.

Hindu Scholar Haridas Chaudhuri, in his book *Being, Evolution and Immortality* explains that immortality transcends the view of the body as a burden:

"The concept of immortality implies a harmonization of the entire personality and a transformation of the physical organism as an effective channel of expression of higher values. This may be called material immortality (rupantar mukti).

"There are some mystics and spiritual seekers who strengthen and purify their bodies just enough to be able to experience the thrilling touch of the Divine. They use the body as a ladder, by which the pure spiritual level—the domain of immortality—is to be reached. On attaining that level, the body is felt as a burden, as a prison house, as a string of chains that holds one in bondage. Dissociation from this last burden of the body is considered a sine qua non for total liberation. Continued association with the body is believed to be the result of the residual trace of ignorance (avidya lesa). When the residual trace of ignorance is gone, the spirit is set free from the shackles of the body.

"The above view is based upon a subtle misconception about the purpose of life and the significance of the body. The body is not only a ladder that leads to the realm of immortality, but also an excellent instrument for expressing the glory of immortality in life and society. It is capable of being thoroughly penetrated by the light of the spirit. It is capable of being transformed into what has been called the 'Diamond Body.' As a result of such transformation, the body does not appear any more to be a burden upon the liberated self. It shines as the Spirit made Flesh. It functions as a very effective instrument for creative action and realization of higher values in the world. It is purged of all inner tension and conflict. It is liberated from the anxiety of repressed wishes. It is also liberated from the dangerous grip of the death impulse born of self-repression. Mystics who look upon the body as a burden suffer from the anxiety of self-repression and the allurement of the death wish.

"Material immortality means decisive victory over both of these demons. It conquers the latent death instinct in man, and fortifies the Will to live as long as necessary, as a channel of expression of the Divine. It also liquidates all forms of self-suppression and self-torture and self-mutilation. As a result the total being of an individual becomes strong and steady, whole and healthy. There is a free flow of psychic energy. It is increasingly channeled into ways of meaningful self-expression. Under the guidance of the indwelling light of the Eternal, it produces increasing manifestation of the Spirit *in* Matter."

—Haridas Chaudhuri

Aliveness Affirmations

40 Beatitudes by Leonard Orr:

1. My mind is centered in Infinite Intelligence that knows my good. I am one with the creative power that is materializing all my desires.
2. All the cells of my body are daily bathed in the perfection of my Divine Being.
3. I now have enough time, energy, wisdom, and money to accomplish all my desires.
4. I am always in the right place at the right time, successfully engaged in the right activity.
5. I now receive assistance and cooperation from all people necessary to achieve my desired goals.
6. My days are filled with mental and physical pleasures.
7. I now give and receive love freely.
8. The more I win, the better I feel about letting others win; the better I feel about letting others win, the more I win. Therefore, I win all the time.
9. I daily make valuable contributions to the aliveness of myself, of others and of humanity.
10. I no longer have to ask permission to do the things I know should be done.
11. I now feel exhilarated and wonderful all of the time!
12. I do not suffer in order to get happiness.
13. My goodness keeps hanging around. Just because something is good does not mean it has to go away.
14. All good things never end; they just keep getting richer.
15. I now feel sweet, joyous peace.
16. I am an ever-flowing spring of aliveness.

I find the following ones particularly beautiful:

17. I am alive now, therefore my life urges are stronger than my death urges. As long as I continue strengthening my life urges, I will go on living in health and youthfulness.
18. Life is eternal. I am life. My mind is the thinking quality of life itself and is eternal. My physical body is also eternal; therefore, my living flesh has a natural tendency to live forever in perfect health and youthfulness.
19. My physical body is a safe and pleasurable place for me to be. The entire universe exists for the purpose of supporting my physical body and providing a pleasurable place for me to express myself.
20. I am commissioned by the Infinite One (God) to assist in the scheme of creation.
21. I am cooperating in the evolution of life, and in so doing my soul and body and their infinite possibilities are progressing in proportion to my desire to use all my powers and possibilities in spirit and in truth.
22. My physical organism is my natural universe, over which I alone will rule. It is my material cloak, or garment, through which I will manifest the powers of divine nature. It is my fundamental servant.
23. I am progressing rapidly toward the conscious subjugation of matter and the complete lordship over all basic elements of life, which exist only by my permission as peaceful and obedient servant.
24. All the cells, tissues, and organs in my body are now youthing according to my desires.
25. The divine alchemist within is transforming the appearance of my body to express its eternal youthfulness.
26. My body is youthing; It daily expresses more health and strength.
27. I am now starting the youthing process. Each birthday I will become a year younger.
28. I have eternal life: My body totally renews itself as long as I like.

29. I am cooperating in the progressive evolution of creation; the entire universe supports and assists my life and goals. My soul and body, with their infinite possibilities, are progressing in accordance with my desires. I now use all of my powers and possibilities in spirit and in truth.
30. My physical body is my most valuable possession.
31. The more I am good to myself, the more I enrich my aliveness.
32. I do not give my body a chance to self-destruct.
33. Each one of my cells grows in perfect youth, becoming more alive and energetic every day. Each cell replaces itself with a finer, purer, more perfect cell.
34. The only germs that can harm me are the germs of bad ideas.
35. My body is not one with pain; I can therefore let go of pain anytime I want.
36. As one with God, I have the ability to substitute health for sickness.
37. I treat myself well and increase my joy, and thus increase the joy of those around me.
38. My body is a loving servant, which is trying to teach me to give up my false ideas so I can enjoy eternal life and all its pleasures.
39. Infinite intelligence is healing my body.

And this one is from *A Course in Miracles*, Lesson 163:

40. There is no death, the Son of God is free.

The most tenacious thought that needs to be corrected is the thought, "I am separate from God." Next in line is our personal lie. Next in line is the thought, "Death is inevitable." These three thoughts alone cause endless suffering until they are transmuted to neutrality. The following affirmations help with this:

- My Creator and I are one.
- I am a child of God, now and always.
- I am constantly connected to Divine Intelligence.
- It is not possible for me to be separate from my Source.

- My Divine Connection brings me endless Peace and Joy.
- I am innocent.
- I now accept my complete innocence in this lifetime and in all former lifetimes.
- Even though I made a mistake, I love and accept myself.
- I am an innocent child of God, as are all people.
- I always extend my innocence to others and see the same innocence in them.
- I am Life.
- I replace all thoughts of death with Life.
- God's will for me is immortal Life.
- I am as God created me now.
- My life is unlimited and infinite.
- I am Love. Love never ends. It is immortal. Therefore, I am immortal.

The following affirmation written by Leonard Orr has helped thousands. I recommend that you memorize it and master it through meditation. Mastering this affirmation now is like having your own personal guardian angel to protect you:

> *I am alive now, therefore my life urges are stronger than my death urges. As long as I strengthen my life urges and weaken my death urges, I will go on living in increasing health and youthfulness.*

Babaji The Immortal Master

Babaji, also named Sri Sri 1008 Bhagwan Herakhan Wale Baba, is a Maha Avatar who manifested from the Divine Mother herself. In other words, he materialized a body directly and was not born from the womb of a woman but rather from the Divine Mother's womb. He has retained his physical form for centuries, perhaps for millenniums. The deathless Babaji is an avatara, which means "the descent of divinity into flesh." His spiritual state is beyond comprehension. He dematerialized a form in 1922 and materialized another form in 1970.

I first met Babaji in this life in 1977, and I have been trained by him personally ever since. The founder of rebirthing, Leonard Orr, calls Babaji the "Father of Rebirthing." His presence is all around this work all the time and it is He who asked us to emphasize the Divine Mother energy more to balance things. He is seen by people only when He desires. He has appeared to many clients during their sessions and we take people to his ashram in India every Spring. Leonard Orr acknowledges Babaji as giving him the inspiration for rebirthing. I acknowledge Babaji for that also and for inspiring me to create The Loving Relationships Training® at about the same time as rebirthing came in. And now, I acknowledge Him and the Divine Mother for inspiring Liberation Breathing®. Also, I acknowledge Babaji for inspiring me to write all 20 books I have done so far, and for making my life a miracle.

In 1922, Old Herakhan Baba, the former manifestation of Babaji, ended one lifetime by disappearing into the convergence of the Gauri and Kali Rivers on the Nepalese border before a group of followers. In 1970, when He reappeared, He climbed to the top of Mount Kailash, across from the small village of Haidakahn where he sat for 45 days in perfect lotus position, without sleeping or eating or drinking.

This eyewitness account of the event comes from G. Reichel Verlag's book, *Babaji, Message from the Himalayas*: "One night (it was June 1970), my father, who had been dead for over 25 years appeared to me in a dream…" so Chandramani begins his narrative. He lives in a village near Haidakhan and was the first person to meet Baba Haidakhan again knowing full well who he was and accordingly pay his respects. "My father had a message for me," Chandramani takes up his narrative again, "that Baba Haidakhan had manifested again as a young man and was presently to be found in the Haidakhan cave. My father told me to go straight away to the cave for darshan [holy meeting] and pay homage to him, because he was truly Baba Haidakhan, beyond any doubt. He also warned me to ignore the critical opinions of other people, whoever they may be, and never to forsake Babaji, come what may.

"When I awoke, it was still very early (4 o'clock) but I set out immediately for the cave. Inside I found a venerable old man sitting in meditative composure by the dim light of a small oil lamp. I noticed he had a long white beard and his body was draped with a white cloth. He looked at me and said: My child, go home and come back in three days.

"Well, I did go home, but returned immediately with a jug full of milk. You can imagine my astonishment when I entered the cave and found, not a venerable old man, but a serene young man, about 22 years of age if that, with long dark hair…He accepted the milk and very slowly drank some. Then he said to me: 'Don't tell anyone what you have seen here.'

"The next two days I went to the cave again, but he wasn't there. On the third day I found him in the temple on the hilltop on the other side of the Gautama Ganga [River], opposite the cave. He remained there for fifteen days, and after that he climbed to the top of Mount Kailash and sat cross legged in full lotus position for forty-five days without moving. You could tell he was absorbed in the most profound meditation.

"I was up there with him the whole time, and not once did I see him get up for anything, not even to take a bath. He remained sitting absolutely still. When he finally came out of this deep meditation, I asked him how he proposed to take a bath since there was not a drop of water in sight, and he answered: 'I shall command the wind to bring me water' and the next thing I see is his lovely long hair dripping wet and his divine body covered in moisture." (pp. 47-48)

— Chandramani

Babaji can assume any form He wishes and can change that form at any time. Since he is an immortal spirit avatar who has the ability to dematerialize and rematerialize at will, he can turn his body into a ball of light and travel anywhere in the universe. His physical bodies can change rapidly, partly because he processes his devotees' karmas rapidly. He can also drop a body whenever he feels like it for whatever purpose. On one occasion after he "left," he appeared to me as a beautiful woman walking on air—as beautiful as I had ever seen in any lifetime…the Divine Mother he/she was!

Being around his body was very dramatic. It took me two years to recover from the first sight I had of him! However, one of his astounding *leelas* (divine play) is his power to bless and guide yogis and devotees all over the world without his actual presence. While Babaji was physically present with us, and while we would be standing right there with him, he would also be busy all over the world at the exact same time! The glory of him is greater than the mind can grasp. At times when he walked he left no footprints. He would run up a hill as though wings were attached to his feet. Some people who picked him up reported that he weighed almost nothing. Other times he would be so heavy they could not pick him up (such was his divine play)!

No scholar has been able to really say where Babaji comes from or where he goes. One book in Hindi describes the cosmic significance of every part of his body. He seemed to carry the earth in his belly. When we asked what was in his belly, he would say, "The sun, the moon, the earth, and the stars," or he would say he was pregnant with five babies: earth, air fire, water, and ether. From time to time certain symbols appeared on the soles of his feet, which are known and identified in the Indian spiritual tradition as cosmic marks:

- the Sanskrit letter OM (the sound of creation, essence of the universe)
- the Shesh Nag (five-hooded snake, symbolizing the five senses and five elements)
- conch shells (symbolizing the element of sound used in worship)
- trident (the emblem of sovereignty and symbol of Shiva)
- head of a bull (Lord Shiva's attendant and vehicle)
- a swastika (ancient Vedic symbol of peace and success, NOT to be confused with the symbol subverted and reversed in direction used by Hitler in WWII)
- peacock
- lotus flower
- bow
- chakra or wheel

- the crescent moon and all the signs of the zodiac
- the planetary system with sun and moon at its center

These marks fulfill the predictions delivered long ago that when Shiva was next to appear in human form, he would have these symbols, and a scar on his lower right leg and upper left arm (which he did).

His spiritual significance has always been beyond comprehension. "Shiva" means eternally happy and auspicious; the God without second who has been moving in this world in his form since creation, watchful for eternity over the welfare of mankind and the universe. He is described as ever-pure, changeless, all pervading, eternal, the immortal essence of the universe, the embodiment of the wisdom…capable of doing anything at any moment or any magnitude.

To visit any of his ashrams is a gift. Once you do, your life will never ever be the same. However, the value of your visit will be determined by your own personal purification. We are happy to take you to India to his main ashram where we attend the Divine Mother Festival every spring. If you are interested, visit LiberationBreathing.com. The Divine Mother's India Quest is the most powerful thing we could ever offer. *Why not think about going to India to visit Babaji's home, and meditate in his cave with Markus and me?* You might also consider going to Babaji's powerful ashram in America in Colorado (www.babajiashram.org or info@babajiashram.org) or other ashram sites worldwide.

A Vow of Immortality

If you are serious about ascension and immortality, it is advisable that you take an actual *vow*. A vow is alive. It is a dimension beyond an affirmation. It involves calling a witness. You go to a holy spot and you take this vow with another immortalist. You set up an altar and you make a statement out loud such as: *"I dedicate my true will to the attainment of physical immortality and the goal of ascension."* Then you write down ten reasons why it is great to be alive. Read those reasons to the altar. On the altar you might want to have pictures of the immortal masters such as Babaji, Jesus, St. Germain, etc.

Ascension is a leap from third dimensional reality to fifth dimensional reality. It is going beyond birth and death. You do not think your way to this dimension. It is a very heart-centered path. In the Bible you will find this statement: "Ye who are grateful for all things, your body shall be filled with light and ye shall comprehend all things."

I have learned that all of humanity is on the path of ascension. But there is a vast difference between those who are consciously on the path of ascension and those who are not. Those who are conscious are functioning at quite a different frequency. God realization becomes their very reason for being.

There is even such a thing as the "Melchizedek Priesthood." The members are those teachers (male and female) from all traditions who are devoted to spiritually immortalizing the body. They are beings of great peace. They can translate their bodies to incorruptible bodies. Melchizedek is called the King of Peace. In Hebrews 7:1-3 you can read about him in the Bible. It says, "Melchizedek has no father, no mother, no lineage, his years have no beginning and no end. He is the Son of God and is a Priest for all time." This means that he materialized his body.

Babaji's High Priest, Shastriji, told me in person that Melchizedek was one form of Babaji. I had no trouble accepting that. After all, my guru would never want the karma of lying to me. Furthermore, I know Babaji has been dematerializing and rematerializing for eons. Shastriji also told me Babaji could have as many 108 bodies at the same time!

An important work to read is *Life and Teachings of the Masters of the Far East* by Baird T. Spalding. Comprised of five volumes, it is the story of eleven American scientists and scholars who studied and lived with the masters in the Himalayas for 3-1/2 years in the 1890s. They had lived with the masters for a whole year before they realized the Masters had been materializing their food! The mind at first cannot integrate it. I know a man who went to India and saw 12 masters levitating. It took him 12 years to remember that he even saw that!

You might say: "Yes, but these high hopes are really just reserved for the masters." You have to think differently. Today, everyone needs to become a spiritual master. If you have the ability to destroy your physical body (which takes a whole lot of effort) you can just as well preserve your physical body, which is actually easier because you are in the flow and not contrary to it. However, if you believe that death is inevitable you are in the process of dying right now!

Or you might say, "A hundred years is all I can take!" That statement springs from a deep-rooted belief in suffering and limitation. You then have not yet experienced the fullness of health, joy, wisdom, peace, and love. It is amazing to me how many people do *not* want to prolong their life.

Once in India Babaji said to everyone in the temple the following: "If you want physical immortality, then go down to the river and spend all night meditating on the fire and say the following mantra." I thought, "WOW!" and grabbed my stuff. Only four of us got up however. Then I thought, "What is wrong with these people, don't they want to *live*?" Later I found out that most did not even hear that. Then it started raining and two backed out. Amazingly, I had the most profound experience of my life. I felt sad they all missed it.

What kills people? Some people are said to die by drowning and yet there are yogi masters who stay submerged for days without air and come out unharmed. We could say that falling from heights kills people. *What height is high enough?* One person dies by falling off a step, another person might die by falling off a roof. In *From Here to Greater Happiness*, there is a true story of two drunks who fell of out a forty story window and walked away unharmed because they did not know they fell out! Then there is the Lufthansa stewardess who fell forty-five thousand feet out of an exploding airplane and lived through it. If a person's unconscious death urge is strong enough, he can trip over a carpet and die!

Here is what *A Course in Miracles* has to say: "Death is not your Father's will, nor yours. The death penalty is the ego's ultimate goal, for it truly believes that you are a criminal deserving of death. The death penalty never leaves the ego's mind; for that is what it always reserves for you in the end. It will torment you while you live, but its hatred is not satisfied until you die. As long as you feel guilty you are listening to the voice of the ego, which tells you that you have been treacherous to God and therefore deserve death. You will think that death comes from God and not from the ego, because by confusing yourself with the ego, you believe that you want death!"

"When you are tempted to the desire for death, remember that I did not die! [Jesus talking]. Would I have overcome death for myself alone? And would eternal life have been given to one of the Father's sons unless He had also given it to you? When you learn to make me manifest, you will never see death." (T-12 VII 15:1)

My Perspectives on Immortality

My mother always said to me that *life is a miracle*, so I honor life. It took me so long to work out my karma and "case" that I sought to find out what it feels like to have *pure life* (life without death). The more I worked out my death urge, the more life became for me an amusement park. The knowledge of physical immortality became the single most exciting thing for me other than meeting my master Babaji. This knowledge has saved my life many times and given me another chance. I feel it would be a waste for me to check out now with all the knowledge I have to share. I did have many tests and initiations on this subject, however.

When I first started writing chapters and books on this subject, I went through acute aging. I started aging at age 33. I did not like it at all. I was glad I was young and strong enough to process it! I wrote about that in my book *Healing and Holiness*. I went through arthritis, rheumatism, senility, you name it. It was actually very interesting. I would not trade that learning experience for anything. The hardest times for me were when family members died. It took years for me to process what came up for me after my father died, after my sister died, and especially after my mother died. One of the reasons I did not die after those experiences was I was a rebel. It is harder if you are a conformist.

When Leonard Orr and I began rebirthing there was very little agreement on the subject of immortality. But Leonard blazed forward. Every month those of us beginning as rebirthers would meet for one full 12-hour day. We all agreed to read nothing but immortalist literature for one whole year. Each month we would give book reports to each other on what we had read. Now that I think of it, it was a brilliant idea because it made us strong and we were able then to go out in the world as trailblazers. It gave me tremendous fortitude. I dare you to try it. If you stay on the path of ascension, constantly raising the vibrations of your mind and body to more and more light, there is a point where you actually do stop aging!

In India it is said that only the Divine Mother can give you the boon (blessing) of physical immortality. Through this book and the path of Liberation Breathing®, we impart the Divine Mother's gift to you.

Dedication From Babaji's Cave

SONDRA: We are now offering our book, *Liberation Breathing: The Divine Mother's Gift*, up to the Divine Mother Herself, and Babaji, in Babaji's cave where He actually materialized His body. So we ask for a big blessing. We have done our best with this book; we have worked really hard, and we turn it over for the marketing to be done in an easy way that we don't know about. And that will come to us, that we have now finished the book and Babaji is happy about it.

MARKUS: Well, I think I would like to mention the potential this book has to transform people's lives. We were really given the direction from the Divine Mother to call the breathing **Liberation Breathing**®; and it was confirmed by Muniraj [Babaji's main disciple], so we felt it was directly from Babaji and the Divine Mother for him to confirm it, and then he gave us the date when we would start using that name. For almost the last five years we have been teaching **Liberation Breathing**® in our seminars and putting it out there; and getting the proper website, and the proper social media. So we feel like we have done the background, the groundwork, and now the book is very close to being published; and we started our own publishing company: **Immortal Ray Productions**—and that can be the way we get the books and our message out.

So we are here in the Cave, and would like to thank all those people who helped to bring us this far —all of our teachers here in India; all of our students; people who helped us edit the book; and a special thanks to Lia Schultz for pushing us forward in **Immortal Ray Productions**.

SONDRA: Yes, I'd like to say a prayer for our organizers around the world that they like this book and are willing to spread it. And I have this vision that people will get a free copy in the seminar. And I kind of like that vision because then I know they will tell other people about it, and word of mouth is really important. But I think we have to let go now, and not try to manipulate the next step, because we do not actually know the next step. We have to turn that over to the Divine Mother and Babaji because we really don't have any idea what to do next. Maybe it will come to us in this Navaratri [this nine-day Divine Mother Festival in which we are participating]. I am open for that. But I offer this book up for the next step so it can be extremely successful in the world.

MARKUS: We are also offering up **Liberation Breathing**® as a process people can use to come to know who they really are, let go of their past, let go of their negative thoughts, and be their True Self. That is what liberation is all about—being your True Self—and that is why we take a life, to basically be who we are and express our Divinity. *What better place could we launch and initiate this book, but in Babaji's Cave?*

SONDRA: Yes, it's a miracle that we really have it in our hands while we came here [in the cave]. We are on the first day of the New Year for India, and they told us today at the fire ceremony that was very auspicious this year, this Navaratri. So I am asking for immense success with this book; I am asking for the right people to put it out there. I am so happy and grateful that all those people necessary are coming forward to bring about that desired result; I am so happy and grateful that marketing is handled; I am so happy and grateful that people love the book; and I am so happy and grateful that we can offer it to the Divine Mother and Babaji as our work, like our baby, kind of. It feels good to do that here in the Cave.

MARKUS: This is coming off of our trip to Israel. And we were also in the Cave where Jesus was buried and resurrected. So I think our work in Israel will continue. And somehow, this "being in Babaji's Cave" feels like a similar, similar energy. We need this energy to go out to Israel, or any place that we're teaching around the world. We take the Cave with us. *And the Cave…what does the Cave represent?* It represents our pure Self, our divine Self, our ability to manifest from our Divine Will. That is Babaji's message—that you are Divine—and all you have to remember is Truth, Simplicity, Love and Service. With the pillars of that lifestyle you realize your Divine Self. And that is what **Liberation Breathing**® is all about. It is just another tool along the way—a major tool—to use your most essential element, your breath, to discover your True Self.

SONDRA: Yes, I must say I am feeling very protected on this mission right now, and going forward with our mission. I feel a light around me that is a protection, that prevents me from having any fear of coming out. If I thought I had any, it is gone right now. That is the good thing I am getting. I can move forward with the Divine Mother protecting you and me…and there is nothing to fear. I don't want to let anything get in the way of us moving forward.

MARKUS: Right. And we have other books ready to go as well, so this is just the first step in our work really being out there as a couple, because we wrote this book together. You had written many books by yourself, but when we got together it was a totally different energy. It's a manifestation of a loving relationship, and that is what we want to write about. It's a demonstration for other people to see how they can live their life in harmony without conflict in a relationship, a holy relationship.

SONDRA: I'm feeling happy that Babaji arranged it so we could be here in the cave alone right now. There might be some people waiting outside, but there is nobody else in here but us. And that feels really nice. So this is some kind of initiation for me to have branched out from the old *rebirthing* model, and the old *rebirthing* energy; having the courage to change the name; and having the courage to talk about the Divine Mother in public, and Babaji. I feel good about that, even on the media. I don't really care if people have a problem with it. I don't want to water myself down because people are hesitant to understand what Babaji is, or what the Divine Mother is. I think we can teach them and show them…and this book can do it.

MARKUS: I want to acknowledge we are here in the Cave where Babaji manifested [a body]. And this is like the womb of the Divine Mother. And I want to acknowledge that this place on earth, where we are sitting, if you could say, "Is there any Source from which your work comes?"…this would have to be the highest Source—Babaji and the Divine Mother, and Their Energy that emanates from this Cave. So, I think it is very fitting that we are laying this book at Their feet in this Cave, initiating the book. And initiating a new beginning to our work, starting here. And everything after this, we acknowledge that Babaji and the Divine Mother, and Jesus of *A Course in Miracles*, are the Source of our work.

SONDRA: And They are moving ahead of us. They are moving ahead of us to open a way. They are carving a path for us. That is the feeling I have…there is an open path that we can go down, that They provided for us. And people now have this window of opportunity.

MARKUS: OK. As we say….

SONDRA & MARKUS: 'Bole Baba Ki Jai!' Thank You.

Ode #365: From the Tomb of Jesus to Babaji's Cave

Divine Mother who resides in Jerusalem, would you have me be a witness to the most sacred spot in the Western world, as You lead me into the cave where He was, Your Son Jesus, on the day of His death. I saw the slab where he laid, and in that charged air of resurrection did I see with different eyes. On that day of rising did You infuse His body to life, turning a tomb into a cavern of compassion, proving there is no death that cannot be overcome. O great Mother of Immortal Life would I invoke you in my Self. Come into me and cleanse me of all impurities. Take me to the cave of resurrection and bring all my systems of thought, mind, and body into total alignment with my spirit in You. I am the Son You love as well, in my true Identity. Be with me every second of my day, in full and blazing awareness of Who I am. Take me into the inner chamber of this transmutation; I am ready to serve You in my true Self. Transport me across continents and oceans to the other most sacred cave on earth…to Babaji's cave in the Himalayan foothills, to that center of the universe of infinite Love, Haidakhan, the most sacred spot in the Eastern world. In there did Your spark of creation turn into immense light, and there did Your Son Haidakhan Babaji manifest a body from Your pure Shakti of total illumination. From Jesus' tomb to Babaji's cave am I given this holy vision of Your absolute truth of immortal life. I sit in the darkness of Your Love out of which my lord Shiva was born into form, not through the womb of a woman, but from the universal energy of Your ever present will to assist humanity. I am in awe of your Power. I am at Your feet requesting my awakening out of the tomb of death into the light-filled cave of immortal Life.

—Markus Ray
Odes to the Divine Mother

Figure 15. Sondra Ray and Markus, Wedding Day in Haidakhan, April 4, 2009

Victory to the Divine Mother!
Victory to the Divine Father!
Victory to the Client!
Victory to the Liberation Breathworker!
Victory to the Breath of Life Itself!

We lay the whole process of Liberation Breathing
at your feet Divine Mother and Divine Father.
Thank you for continuing to teach us how to perfect it.

Love,

Sondra Ray & Markus Ray

Book List—Recommended Reading

Birth
Birth Without Violence — Fredrick LeBoyer
Babies Remember Birth — David Chamberlain
Ideal Birth — Sondra Ray
Birth Reborn — Michele Odent
Primal Connections — Elizabeth Noble
The Continuum Concept: In Search of Happiness Lost — Jean Liedloff

Conception and Pre-Conception
The Child of Your Dreams — Laura Huxley
The Secret Life of the Unborn Child — Thomas Verney
Voices From The Womb — Michael Gabriel

Family and Relationships
Brothers and Sisters: The Order of Birth in the Family — Karl Konig
Loving Relationships I and II — Sondra Ray
The Birth Order Effect for Couples — Cliff Isaacson and Meg Schneider
The Family — John Bradshaw
The Loving Relationships Treasury — Sondra Ray

Film and Video
Birth Into Being — Elena Tonetti-Vladimirova
The Miracle of Life — Lennart Nilsson
What Babies Want — Debby Takikawa

Healing
Healing and Holiness — Sondra Ray
Messages from the Body: Their Psychological Meaning —Michael Lincoln
Quantum Healing — Deepak Chopra
The Dynamic Laws of Healing — Catherine Ponder
You Can Heal Your Life — Louise Hay

Metaphysic Basics
As A Man Thinketh — Napolean Hill
From Here to Greater Happiness — Joel and Champion Teutsch
New Beginnings Book Two — Esther and Jerry Hicks
Resurrection — Neville Goddard
The Art of Deliberate Creation — Esther and Jerry Hicks
The Magic — Rhonda Byrne
The Power — Rhonda Byrne
The Secret — Rhonda Byrne

Money and Prosperity
Ask and It is Given — Esther and Jerry Hicks
Money is My Friend — Phil Laut
The Dynamic Laws of Prosperity — Catherine Ponder
Think and Grow Rich — Napolean Hill

Past Lives
Many Lives, Many Selves — Brian Weiss
Other Lives, Other Selves — Roger Wolger
We Were Born Again To Be Together — Dick Sutphen

Rebirthing
Birth and Relationships — Sondra Ray and Bob Mandel
Breath and Spirit — Gunnell Minnet
Breathing — Michael Sky
Breathing In Light and Love — Jim Morningstar
Celebration of Breath — Sondra Ray
Rebirthing — Dieke Begg
Rebirthing In The New Age — Sondra Ray and Leonard Orr
Rebirthing Made Easy — Colin Sisson
Rebirthing: The Science of Enjoying All Of Your Life — Jim Leonard and Phil Laut

Sexuality and Incest
I Deserve Love — Sondra Ray
Sexual Evolution — Rhonda Levand
Silently Seduced: Revised and Updated — Kenneth Adams and Patrick Carnes

Physical Immortality
Being, Evolution, and Immortality — Haridas Chaudhuri
Beyond Mortal Boundaries — Annalee Skarin
Breaking The Death Habit — Leonard Orr
How To Be Chic and Fabulous and Live Forever — Sondra Ray
Immortality: How Science is Extending Your Life Span — Ben Bova
Living Without Death — James Strole
Paradise 1 — Alan Harrington
Physical Immortality — Leonard Orr
Psychological Immortality — Jerry Giles
Secrets of Eternity — Annalee Skarin
Star Signs — Linda Goodmann
Stop Dying and Live Forever — Stanley Spears
Tao of Health, Longevity, and Immortality: The Teachings of Immortals — Eva Wong
Taoism: The Quest for Immortality — John Blofeld
The Alchemyst: The Secrets of the Immortal Nicholas Flamel Series — Michael Scott
The Art of Everlasting Life — Robert Coon
The Common Sense of Physical Immortality — Leonard Orr
The Door of Everything — Ruby Nelson
The Fulcanelli Phenomenon — Kenneth Raynor Johnson
The Game of Life — Timothy Leary
The Immortalist — Alan Harrington
The Life and Teachings of the Masters Of The Far East — Baird T. Spaulding
The Mind of the Cells — Satprem
The Path of the Phoenix — Robert Coon
The Rainbow Serpent and the Holy Grail — Robert Coon

The Romeo Error — Lyell Watson
Unveiled Mysteries — Godfre Ray King
Voyage to Avalon — Robert Coon

Spirituality

A Course in Miracles (online version available at acim-search.miraclevision.com)
Amma and Me — Manoharan
Autobiography of a Yogi — Paramahansa Yogananda (available at www.ananda.org)
Celestial Song of Creation — Annalee Skarin
Man Triumphant — Annalee Skarin
Power vs. Force — David Hawkins
Rock Your World with the Divine Mother — Sondra Ray
Shiva Mahavatar Babaji — Pola Churchill
Soul Agreements — Dick Sutphen
The Aquarian Gospel — Levi H. Dowling
The Book of Books — Annalee Skarin
The Book of Mormon and Doctrine of the Covenants — Joseph Smith, Jr.
The Essene Gospels — Translated and edited by Edmond Bordeaux Szekely
The Path of The Mother — Ammachi
The Temple of God — Annalee Skarin
To God the Glory — Annalee Skarin
Transcending The Levels of Consciousness — David Hawkins
Ye are Gods — Annalee Skarin

Notes

Notes

Notes

Notes

About the Authors

Sondra Ray is known as one of the most dynamic spiritual leaders of our day. She is recognized throughout the world as a spiritual teacher, author, rebirther, lecturer, and healer, with a renowned expertise in the area of relationships.

Sondra was launched into international acclaim in the 1970s as one of the pioneers of the Rebirthing Experience. She has trained thousands of people all over the world in the Rebirthing process, and is considered one of the foremost experts on how the birth trauma affects one's body, relationships, career and life. As she puts it, this conscious connected breathing process produces extraordinary healing results. By taking in more Life Force through the breath, limiting thoughts and memories that cause problems and disease are released. Sondra has taken Rebirthing to a new level of effectiveness by invoking the Divine Mother energy into the breathing sessions. Her new expression of this process is called Liberation Breathing®.

Often ordained as the "Mother of Rebirthing," Sondra creates and teaches seminars, including her most popular Loving Relationships Training®. This training has helped thousands of people get clear on their relationships by explaining common negative family patterns and by dissolving these patterns through applying practices of Rebirthing and creative thought. Ray has taken these seminars and trainings around the globe to countries including England, France, Spain, Italy, Germany, Iceland, Ireland, Poland, Sweden, Estonia, Russia, New Zealand, Australia, Singapore, Bali and Japan. She also takes groups to India for annual pilgrimages.

Other seminar subjects she teaches are Liberation Breathing® Intensives, the New Frequency for Relationships, Miracle Consciousness, Spiritual Healing, The Money Seminar, and Physical Immortality. All of these trainings are unique because they all include Rebirthing or Liberation Breathing® as the central method for problem solving and spiritual purification.

Sondra also had the privilege of spending time with the immortal Master, Maha Avatar Haidakahn Babaji, in India on several occasions from 1977-1984, becoming His lifelong student and disciple. For the past 26 years she has led groups to India and introduced hundreds to Haidakahn and the deep spiritual heritage this country has to offer. She leads groups to India every spring to participate in the Navratri, a nine-day spiritual festival dedicated to honoring the Divine Mother, the feminine aspects of the Divine Nature that permeates all Life. Participants are also immersed in the Liberation Breathing® process daily during the India Quest, her most powerful offering of the year.

Sondra Ray currently travels the world teaching, and has a private healing practice with her husband, Markus Ray. People who have worked with them say rebirthing and the Liberation Breathing® process have saved them years of time in their awakening and spiritual evolution. Applying 40 years of metaphysical study, Sondra has helped thousands of people move beyond pain and negative thought patterns to celebrate Life more fully. No matter what Sondra Ray is doing, she is always trying to bring about a higher consciousness. Recently she created "Spiritual Intimacy: The New Frequency for Relationships" training, which she envisions will shift the current paradigm in relationships around the world to a new level of consciousness, free from anger and conflict.

In her formative years before her life mission as a rebirther, teacher and author, Ray earned a B.S. degree in nursing from the University of Florida College of Nursing, and a Master's degree in Public Health and Family Sociology from the University of Arizona. She was trained as a Nurse Practitioner in Obstetrics and Gynecology. Early on she worked in the Peace Corps and was stationed in Peru, which prepared her for world service.

Markus Ray received his training in the arts, holding an MFA in painting. Also a writer and a poet, he brings spirituality and sensuality together in these mediums of expression. Markus speaks in their seminars around the world of the profound modern psychological/spiritual scripture, *A Course in Miracles*. He studied *ACIM* with his master, Tara Singh, for 17 years in order to experience its truth directly. Tara Singh was ordained by Dr. Helen Schucman, the scribe of *A Course in Miracles*, to teach the material to serious students.

Markus' spiritual quest has taken him to India many times, where Muniraj, Babaji's foremost disciple, gave him the name Man Mohan, "the Poet who steals the hearts of the people." In all of his paintings, writings, and lectures Markus creates a quiet atmosphere of peace and clarity that is an invitation to go deeper into the realms of inner stillness and beauty. He teaches with Sondra Ray, and many have been touched by their demonstration of a holy relationship in action. He serves as lecturer, creative director, and coauthor with Sondra Ray, traveling globally to teach on such topics as holy relationships, creativity, miracles, and Divine love. His forthcoming books, *Miracles with My Master, Tara Singh* and *Odes to the Divine Mother*, chronicle the spiritual depth and artistic breadth of Markus as a visionary teacher, painter, and poet for the Aquarian Age.

In 1989, Markus embarked on an extraordinary evolution in his training: "When I met Tara Singh, I knew my destiny was complete. I had found my real teacher in life." For the next 17 years, he studied under spiritual master Tara Singh, a man dedicated to spreading the modern-day scripture and teachings contained within *A Course in Miracles*. Under Mr. Singh's guidance, Markus became particularly attentive to the Holy Encounter or *darshan* experienced in the presence of both modern-day and ancient Holy Beings. It is this holy vision on the face of the Divine that his sacred portraits now capture—imparting a unique blessing and inspiring miracles in the lives of viewers. Markus shares the sublime beauty of his journeys, paintings, and poems at LiberationBreathing.com.

Sondra and Markus were brought together by the grace of their Master, Maha Avatar Haidakahn Babaji. Babaji said, "Markus is my Humbleness. Sondra is my Voice. Together they are my Love." As Ambassadors for Him, their mission is to bring His teaching of "Truth, Simplicity, Love, and Service to Mankind" along with the presence of the Divine Mother to the world through seminars (like the LRT®) and the conscious connected breathing practice of Liberation Breathing®. They are unfolding the plan of Babaji, which is beyond our wildest dreams! Their relationship is a shining example of what is possible through deep ease and no conflict. They introduce students to higher realms through which miracles consciousness becomes a part of daily life.

We Invite You to Contact Us

To share comments or learn more about seminars,
quests, webinars, books, or private Liberation Breathing® sessions with
SONDRA RAY and MARKUS RAY, please write to us at:

LiberationBreathing.com or
ImmortalRay@earthlink.net

CPSIA information can be obtained at www.ICGtesting.com
Printed in the USA
LVOW03*2346090115

422232LV00007B/17/P